THE BOURBON BIBLE

The complete low-down on the spirit of America – **140 bourbons** tried and tested

INCLUDES BOURBON COCKTAIL RECIPES

THE BOURBON BIBLE

The complete
low-down on
the spirit of
America –
140 bourbons
tried and
tested

**INCLUDES
BOURBON
COCKTAIL
RECIPES**

Eric Zandona

With contributions
by Sara L Smith

MITCHELL BEAZLEY

For my wife Tia

An Hachette UK Company
www.hachette.co.uk

First published in Great Britain in 2018 by Mitchell Beazley, a division of
Octopus Publishing Group Ltd
Carmelite House
50 Victoria Embankment
London EC4Y 0DZ
www.octopusbooks.co.uk
www.octopusbooksusa.com

Distributed in the US by Hachette Book Group
1290 Avenue of the Americas
4th and 5th Floors, New York, NY 10104

Distributed in Canada by Canadian Manda Group
664 Annette Sreet, Toronto, Ontario, Canada M6S 2C8

ISBN 978-1-78472-457-3

A CIP catalogue record for this book is available from the British Library.

Printed and bound in China

10 9 8 7 6 5 4 3 2 1

All gallons stated are US gallons

Page 2: Founded by Lincoln Henderson, former Master Distiller of Brown-Forman,
Angel's Envy Distillery opened in 2016 and began producing bourbon and rye
whiskey to supplement and eventually replace their purchased whiskey.

Commissioning Editor Joe Cottington
Senior Editor Pauline Bache
Copy editor Jo Murray
Art Director Juliette Norsworthy
Designer Penny Stock
Picture Research Manager Giulia Hetherington
Picture Researcher Claire Hamilton
Senior Production Controller Allison Gonsalves

Contents

Since the beginning of the 21st century, bourbon has been on a steady climb in popularity. In fact, the past 15 years have seen the spirit soar both in the US and around the world – with countries such as Japan, Australia, Germany and the United Kingdom all developing a taste for bourbon like never before.

But to the uninitiated, the world of bourbon can be a daunting place, with a wealth of unfamiliar terms and techniques. *The Bourbon Bible* aims to help the novice bourbon fan navigate that world, providing an introduction to the history, production and flavours of bourbon for those who are just discovering America's native spirit.

INTRODUCTION

The opening section – **The Basics** – offers the reader a solid foundation for understanding the historical and technical aspects of how bourbon is made and why it tastes the way is does, and decodes the language and terminology found on its labels. The main section of the book – **The Bourbons** – is designed to help you discover your new favourite bourbon (or five), and to give you an insight into why you might like those particular flavours. As well as giving some background information and a thorough taste profile, each bourbon in the book is accompanied by key information on the type of still used, the mash bill and the length of maturation. Far from being a mere catalogue of facts for you to learn and recite as needed, this information is intended to give you an insight into the bourbon itself – to aid you in identifying which bourbons you particularly enjoy the taste of, where those flavours come from and which other bourbons might have similar flavour profiles for you to explore. Finally, **The Cocktails** offers time-honoured drinks that pair perfectly with bourbon and bring out the very best in this wonderful spirit.

Ultimately, through *The Bourbon Bible*, I hope to share my belief that the subjective experience of flavour – not price, popularity or rarity – is the most important reason to drink any particular bourbon. Whatever kind of bourbon you enjoy, use this book to guide you through the wonderful world of flavours that is waiting to be explored.

Right
Bourbon barrels are charred inside an oven at the Brown-Forman Corp. cooperage facility in Louisville, Kentucky.

PART 1

THE BASICS

1

Much has been written about the history of bourbon whiskey and its place in the wider story of the United States. However, while bourbon is more than 200 years old, the work of fully understanding the part it has played in American history – and where it intersects with the stories of Native Americans, immigrants, women, slaves, politics and religion – has ony just begun.

A QUICK HISTORY OF BOURBON

Distilled spirits have had an important economic and social role in the lives of Americans from the time of the British colonies to the present day. Not long after European colonization of the Americas, settlers tasked themselves with using both local and imported crops to make fermented drinks. In 1587, English settlers at Roanoke made beer from corn because it provided a safe source of water and nutrition – and some alcohol. As the colonies grew, beer from barley and cider from apples and pears became more common and widely available. At the same time, distilleries were popping up to produce spirits from locally grown grain and imported molasses. By 1770, New England had 159 rum distilleries, which made the spirit very inexpensive and popular. Rum became an important part of the triangular trade that moved raw materials, finished goods, weapons and slaves between Africa, the Americas and Europe. However, the American Revolution (1775–83), among other things, made the importation of molasses from the West Indies more expensive so many distillers turned to grain for making whiskey.

Throughout the 18th and 19th centuries American settlers – allowed to claim 160 hectares (400 acres) of land and purchase an additional 400 hectares (1,000 acres) – pushed west into the Appalachian frontier.

Left Puritan colonists in the 17th century drinking from pewter mugs in Massachusetts Bay Colony.

Above Oil painting of President Washington sending troops to put down the Whiskey Rebellion (*see* page 12).

On 31 December 1776, the Virginia General Assembly established that the region beyond the Appalachian Mountains should be designated Kentucky County. Later, in 1780, Kentucky County was split into three smaller counties: Jefferson, Lincoln and Fayette. Fayette County was named after the Marquis de Lafayette who fought alongside the Americans in the American Revolution, and in 1785 Bourbon County was carved out of Fayette County and named in honour of the French royal house of Bourbon, who also provided aid during the war. On 1 June 1792, Kentucky was admitted as the 15th state in the Union. Throughout this period, farmers established homesteads and began planting maize, also called Indian corn. Like their eastern predecessors, these farmers distilled their excess crops into whiskey and began selling and bartering with it.

At this point, questions arise. Who thought to purposely age corn whiskey in charred barrels, and when did this happen? And why was it called bourbon? The truth is, there is no definitive historical evidence that answers these questions. The first printed reference to bourbon whiskey comes from an 1821 advertisement in Bourbon County, and the first written association of bourbon with charred

THE WHISKEY REBELLION

While corn and barley were grown throughout the newly formed United States, rye was the most popular grain for farming and for whiskey. Farmers on the frontier of western Pennsylvania and other states found that it was easier to distil their rye into whiskey and sell or barter with it than attempt to cart it hundreds of miles to the larger population centres. However, in 1791, George Washington passed an excise tax on distilled spirits to help pay off the country's significant debt from the American Revolution. Farm distillers on the frontier, who often lacked cash, resented this and attempted to evade the tax. In 1794, a revolt broke out when US Marshals attempted to enforce payment of the tax. The home of tax inspector John Neville was burned down and in response President George Washington called up 13,000 militiamen and rode into Pennsylvania to squash the so-called Whiskey Rebellion. This was an important turning point in the history of the United States, demonstrating the power of the Federal government and its willingness to enforce its laws. The excise tax remained in effect until 1802 when Thomas Jefferson took office as the third president of the United States.

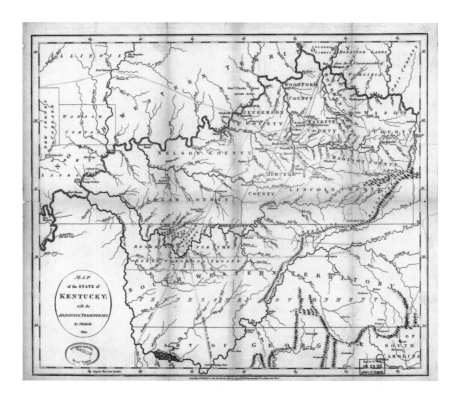

barrels came in 1826 when a Lexington grocer requested whiskey stored in "burnt" barrels. However, these references only point to the fact that by the 1820s it was already well established that there was a whiskey coming out of Kentucky known as bourbon, famed for being stored in charred barrels.

Without direct evidence of when and who first stored corn whiskey in charred barrels and called it bourbon, historians have tried to piece together the most plausible answers. The most repeated – and probably incorrect – answer given is that Elijah Craig, a Baptist minister, invented bourbon in 1789. While Craig was a distiller, among other things, there is no indication that his whiskey was any different from his neighbours' and the first reference to his invention of bourbon does not materialize until 1874.

What seems more likely is that there was no single inventor of bourbon, but many. It is certain that in the late

Above Kentucky State and Adjoining Territories, 1794.

18th century almost all farmers produced some amount of whiskey from their excess grain. Barrels were the most common medium in which to ship goods, and it was also a common practice to recycle barrels. If one wanted to reuse a barrel without absorbing the odours and flavours of the previous contents, it was known that you could simply char the inside to neutralize the barrel. Given these historical facts it seems likely that multiple farmers distilled a mash of corn and other grains and put the resulting whiskey into barrels they had charred to remove previous flavours. When these whiskeys were sold down the river, it was probably noticeable that the spirit from charred barrels had a unique and particularly pleasant flavour compared to whiskey matured in raw or toasted barrels. As a result, it is likely that demand for this type of whiskey grew. Without more historical research, we cannot know for certain if bourbon whiskey was named after the county or the famous New Orleans street, but at present it seems more likely it was referencing the county, especially since the first printed reference to it comes from Bourbon County, Kentucky, and not New Orleans.

Right Smoke rises from bourbon barrels after being charred inside an oven.

MOUNT VERNON DISTILLERY

In 1797, after serving two terms as president, George Washington returned home to Virginia and, at the prompting of Scottish farm manager James Anderson, built a distillery at Mount Vernon to make whiskey from some of his excess grain. Anderson and six slaves made brandy and whiskey distilled from a mash of 60% rye, 35% corn and 5% barley. His common whiskey was distilled twice and sold for 50 cents per gallon (about 13 cents per litre) and a more expensive special whiskey was distilled four times and sold for $1 per gallon (about 26 cents per litre). In 1799, Washington sold 10,500 gallons (39,750 litres) of whiskey, making him the largest and most profitable distiller in Virginia. However, this success was short-lived, coming to an end when the distillery was closed after Washington's death in December 1799.

Throughout the first half of the 19th century, bourbon steadily grew in popularity and distribution, in part because of several improvements to the fermentation process that helped maintain quality. In 1818, the first recorded reference to a distiller using what's known as the sour mash process (*see* page 27) appears. Catherine Carpenter of Casey County, Kentucky, put a portion of a fully fermented batch of mash back into a fresh mash to begin fermentation. Whether she or other distillers at the time knew why this worked is unclear but the result was fewer spoiled fermentations, and improved quality and consistency in flavour and attenuation (the ability of yeast to convert all the available sugar to alcohol).

By the 1850s the process of making bourbon had significantly improved, in no small part due to the work of Dr James C. Crow, for whom Old Crow Bourbon is named. Born in Inverness, Scotland, Crow studied chemistry and medicine at the University of Edinburgh before moving to Kentucky in the 1820s. In 1835, Dr Crow was working at the Glenns Creek Distillery in Woodford County, Kentucky, and began refining the sour mash process and using his training to better understand the process of making bourbon, why certain practices worked and how to improve the flavour and quality of his bourbon through science. As a result of this work, Dr Crow helped to create what we know as bourbon today.

Daniel Webster visits his friend James Crow

Senator Webster, he of the golden tongue and the good life, though Old Crow such a work of art, he visited Dr. Crow at the distillery. The great orator ringingly pronounced Crow's whiskey "the finest in the world"—according to historical archives.

Taste the Greatness of

OLD CROW
America's Preferred Bourbon

James Crow created his bourbon masterpiece 124 years ago—and history beat a path to his door. Today 86 proof Old Crow is favored by more Americans than any other bourbon—because it is still the perfect formula for Kentucky bourbon!

LIGHT · MILD · 86 PROOF
KENTUCKY BOURBON

"The Greatest Name in Bourbon"

THE OLD CROW DISTILLERY COMPANY, FRANKFORT, KENTUCKY. DISTRIBUTED BY NATIONAL DISTILLERS PRODUCTS COMPANY.

By 1865, the American Civil War had curtailed most commercial production of bourbon and slowed its growth. (This pattern would be repeated during World War I and World War II.) After the war, distillers set up shop once again and began producing bourbon. In this post-war period, most bourbon was sold by the barrel and drinkers who did not make their own would buy bourbon at a bar or from a grocer. At a bar, barrels were tapped and the bourbon served to customers; at the grocery, people would bring their own jugs or containers and take the bourbon home. During this period, the practice of diluting the bourbon to make each barrel go further and increase profits was widespread. Middlemen known as rectifiers would buy aged bourbon by the barrel from distilleries and then dilute the bourbon with water. The barrels of this cut bourbon were sold to bars and grocers, who in turn would water down the bourbon again.

By this point the whiskey was so diluted that it had lost a significant amount of its colour, flavour and alcohol. To counteract this, people added neutral alcohol, prune juice or even acid to make the "whiskey" seem more like the real thing. It was also at this time that rectifiers began "inventing" new technologies for rapidly ageing whiskey. In reality, many of these companies were creating imitation whiskey by combining inexpensive neutral spirit, acids, fruit juices, iodine, tobacco and wood extracts to sell as bourbon or other types of whiskey. Not surprisingly, bourbon distillers were unhappy about this bastardization of their whiskey and imitation products sold on the coat-tails of their hard work.

In response, a number of distillers led by Colonel Edmund Haynes Taylor, Jr worked with the US Secretary of the Treasury, John G. Carlisle, to create the Bottled-in-Bond Act of 1897. During the Civil War, the alcohol excise tax was reinstated but collecting the taxes was easier said than done. The Bottled-in-Bond Act provided benefits for distillers who wanted to protect their products from adulteration, the US Treasury who could collect its excise tax and drinkers who wanted authentic bourbon. Although Old Forester Bourbon was the first branded bourbon to be sold solely in sealed bottles in 1870, until the Bottled-in-Bond Act came into force, it and other distillers had no legal recourse to protect their whiskey from tampering.

The Bottled-in-Bond Act allowed distilleries to create a bonded warehouse that was supervised by an on-site US agent, where whiskey or brandy could mature – tax free. Once the spirit reached four years old, the distiller, in the presence of the agent, could vat barrels of the same type (bourbon, rye, malt etc.) produced in the same season (spring season was defined as January–July; autumn season July–January) and reduce the alcohol strength using pure water to 100 proof (50% ABV). Once the spirit was proofed down, it had to be put in bottles clearly marked with the name of the distillery, when it was distilled and when it was bottled before it was sealed with a federal strip stamp, all inside the bonded warehouse. The stamp meant that distillers only had to pay excise tax on the spirit that was actually bottled and left their warehouses. It also indicated to the buying public the high standard under which the spirit was produced, and made it a federal crime to tamper with the bottle or the liquid inside the bottle once it was stamped. This law was a watershed moment – the first-ever US consumer protection law establishing that the government would guarantee the product in the bottle met certain

Below In 1870, most bourbon was sold by the barrel and Old Forester Bourbon was the first bourbon ever bottled at the distillery.

standards and was sold as advertised. Not surprisingly, rectifiers were not happy and immediately challenged the new law in court.

In 1906, Upton Sinclair published *The Jungle*, which exposed the horrid conditions of the US meat packing industry. In response, public outcry for more transparency and truth in labelling led to the passage of the Pure Food and Drug Act at the end of Theodore Roosevelt's presidency. The law allowed for the labelling of pure whiskey, but there was no written definition of what constituted whiskey. In response to pressure from both rectifiers and distillers, President William Howard Taft decided to settle this dispute. In 1909, after six months of deliberation and input from rectifiers and straight whiskey distillers, President Taft established definitions for straight whiskey, blended whiskey and imitation whiskey. The Taft Decision, as it became known, created the basic definition of straight bourbon that we use today: a spirit made from a fermented mash of at least 51% corn distilled to less than 160 proof (80% ABV) and barrelled at less than 125 proof (62.5% ABV) in charred oak barrels and aged for two years. However, bourbon distillers were not completely satisfied, because Taft's decision also created legal definitions for the blended and imitation whiskeys the rectifiers were selling.

At the end of the 19th and beginning of the 20th centuries, economic and social forces in the United States gradually reduced the number of operating bourbon distilleries. The new national market facilitated by the interstate railway system and mass market advertising led to increasing market pressure for consolidation of the bourbon industry, which offered reduced competition and increased profits. At the same time the temperance movement, which started off with the simple message that Americans should moderate their drinking, gradually shifted to the radical proposal that all production, sale and consumption of alcohol should be completely prohibited.

The temperance movement began for good reason. In 1830, the per capita consumption of pure alcohol was 7.1 gallons (26.9 litres) per year – the equivalent of 53.25 bottles of 40% ABV bourbon per year, or slightly more than one bottle a week for every man, woman and child in the United States. By 1916, the message of temperance had worked and the per capita consumption of pure alcohol dropped dramatically to 1.96 gallons (7.42 litres) per year. Then, on 6 April 1917, the United States declared war on Germany and entered World War I. With the declaration of war, US industries – including distilleries – shifted

Below left Temperance Crusade illustration, *c.*1874 depicting the downward spiral of drunkenness.

Below right Political cartoon depicting the greedy fat cat brewer in favour of the "Wet" vote vs the poor women and children who needed the "Dry" vote, *c.*1900s.

production to support the war effort. Instead of making bourbon, patriotic distilleries produced neutral spirits, which were used in munition making.

After the war, conditions for bourbon distillers did not improve a great deal. In 1920, the US Congress ratified the Eighteenth Amendment to the United States Constitution, establishing the national Prohibition of alcohol production, transpiration and sale. Despite the new law, a few distilleries were able to sell their remaining stock of bourbon as "medicinal alcohol" and the Old Fire Copper Distillery (which still operates today as the Buffalo Trace Distillery) was allowed to continue making whiskey for medicinal purposes.

By 1933, when the Twenty-first Amendment repealed Prohibition, much of the country's aged whiskey stock was depleted and the country was in the midst of the Great Depression, making capital for producing and ageing bourbon more difficult to come by. In 1936, Congress passed the Federal Alcohol Administration Act, which created the new legal framework for regulating alcohol production and labelling post-Prohibition. This new law

Below A "Prohibition wagon" draped with banners emphasizing that Prohibition is taken seriously in Arizona, c.1925.

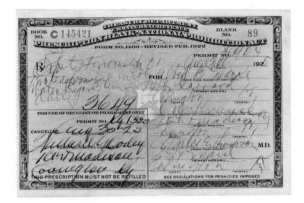

essentially recodified the Taft Decision with one minor change. Without fanfare, the definition of bourbon was amended to include the requirement that the whiskey be aged in new charred oak barrels. The only rationale for this change was that, in the midst of the Great Depression, the requirement to use new barrels for bourbon would essentially create and sustain jobs for coopers. By 1941, the United States was back at war and once again the bourbon industry was called upon to serve its country and produce industrial alcohol for munitions.

By the end of World War II, the economy was booming and things at last started to look up for bourbon producers. Throughout the 1950s and 1960s demand for bourbon grew and distillers responded with large increases in production. In 1964, Congress declared bourbon to be America's Native Spirit. There was, however, an underlying problem. The American palate was undergoing a significant shift in its taste preference for whiskey, in part due to the catalogue of disruptions to bourbon production during the first half of the 20th century. Lighter-style whiskeys such as Canadian Club were growing in popularity, partly because it was widely available during Prohibition and the Great Depression, but also because of a generational shift. Young drinkers were looking for something new, not their parents' or grandparents' old bourbon. By the mid-1970s the bottom had fallen out of the bourbon market as drinkers flocked to light-flavoured whiskeys and vodka, which left bourbon distillers with a huge glut of ageing barrels.

In the 1980s and 1990s, when bourbon popularity was at its nadir, a few important changes took place. In 1984, the

Top During National Prohibition some were allowed to receive a prescription for medicinal alcohol.

Above O.F.C. Whiskey was one of a few bourbons allowed to be sold for medicinal use.

Sazerac Company created Blanton's Single Barrel Bourbon, which was the first modern bourbon ever bottled from one barrel. Then in 1986, Heaven Hill introduced the first "small batch" bourbon (*see* page 40), which at the time was made of bourbon aged for a minimum of 12 years. Three years later in 1989, the first bottling of Old Rip Van Winkle 15-year-old bourbon was released. Soon after, Jim Beam followed suit with four new bourbons to create its small batch collection. All of these innovations were possible because the bourbon industry had slow sales and was sitting on millions of barrels that were only getting older.

By the early 2000s, tastes slowly began to change again. A renewed interest in classic cocktails and the emergence of the craft distilling movement helped to drive more interest in brown spirits in general and bourbon in particular. This rediscovery of bourbon by a new generation of drinkers has continued to grow and today there are more barrels of bourbon ageing in Kentucky than there are people in the state.

Interestingly, this bourbon boom occurred so suddenly that a number of bourbons had to drop their age statements (*see* page 37) or have become very difficult to find due to huge demand. Thankfully, there are still hundreds of bourbon, straight bourbon and bottled-in-bond bourbon brands on the market at all price points and flavour profiles. So while it may be difficult to find that one particular bottle, there are many great brands worth trying.

While the history of bourbon reveals that the good times never last, there also seems to be little slowdown in consumer demand for high-quality bourbon whiskey. So now is the time to go out and get a bottle, or order a glass at your favourite bar, and enjoy one of the world's truly great whiskeys.

Far left above Today, Pappy van Winkle's Family Reserve 15 years old Kentucky Straight Bourbon is one of the most coveted American whiskeys in the market.

Far left In 2016 Constellation Brands acquired the Utah-based High West Distillery and their popular whiskey blends for roughly $160 million (£121 million).

Left In the past decade bourbon cocktails like the Old Fashioned and the Manhattan have once again become very popular.

2

A dictionary definition of bourbon would read something like "A whiskey distilled from a mash consisting of a minimum of 51% corn." While this definition is true, it misses some of the key components of how bourbon is made. These components are not only necessary to meet the carefully protected legal definition created by US Congress, but they also provide information about why bourbon tastes the way it does. Grain selection, water, yeast, fermentation, distillation, maturation, vatting, filtration and proofing all play a role in shaping the flavour profile of each bourbon and inform our experience of drinking and hopefully enjoying it.

FROM CORN TO BOTTLE: HOW BOURBON IS MADE

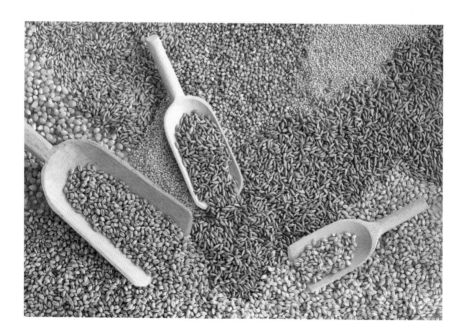

The Key Ingredients

All bourbons begin with the creation of what's known as a mash bill – the selection of particular grains and their ratios that forms the backbone of the flavour profile. The only legal mandate for bourbon with respect to its mash is that it must contain at least 51% corn; malted barley, rye and wheat are the other most commonly used grains.

Corn

Corn is, of course, the defining grain for bourbon and typically accounts for 70–80% of the mash bill, sometimes less. It contributes a sense of sweetness to the final drink, although standard yellow corn can lose many of its other flavour characteristics after ageing in wooden barrels. Most distillers use the standard No. 2 yellow dent corn because of its availability and high starch content, but a few craft distillers have begun using heirloom varieties of white, blue, red and yellow corn in their bourbons. These heirloom varieties offer great flavours for small batch operations – you are not likely to see them used in any of the big Kentucky bourbons any time soon as there is simply not enough being grown and they tend to have lower yields.

Left While whiskey can be made from any grain, bourbon must be made from at least 51% corn.

Above Some craft distillers have begun to make bourbon from heirloom varieties of corn, which produce different flavours to the standard yellow corn.

 Rye and/or Wheat

Rye and wheat are known as flavouring grains, since the taste they impart stays intact over the ageing process. They can account for as little as 8% to as much as 35% of the mash. Rye, the most common flavouring grain, adds dryness and a spicy character to bourbon, which harmonizes beautifully with the sweetness that comes from the corn and the vanilla notes extracted from the barrel. Wheat is the next most common flavouring grain used in bourbon and it is traditionally described as being somewhat sweeter, adding softness and a slight nutty character. This perception of sweetness comes from the fact that wheat does not have the same dryness and spice of rye, so it allows more of the bourbon's natural sweetness to come through. In my experience, wheated bourbons are not necessarily softer or sweeter, but rather wheat allows more of the flavour choices made in the distillation, barrelling and proofing processes to come to the fore.

✚ Malted Barley

Malted barley usually makes up about 5–10% of the mash but plays a significant role, providing all of the enzymes necessary to convert the grains' starch into the simple sugars required to make alcohol. Barley often contributes biscuit and nutty flavours to bourbon, characteristics similar to those you might find in a single malt Scotch whisky.

✚ Water

For good reason one of the main talking points of making bourbon is the water. It can account for up to 60% of what is in the bottle and it plays an important role in fermentation. In Kentucky, they like to brag that their limestone-filtered water is perfect for making bourbon. This claim has a good basis in reality, as water that has worked its way through limestone tends to be low in iron and higher in other minerals. Yeast struggles in high-iron environments and becomes less capable of fermenting sugars into alcohol. Similarly, other minerals serve as micronutrients to the yeast and help keep them happy and healthy longer into the

MAJOR AND MINOR MASH BILLS

There are three major mash bills (rye, high-rye and wheated) used in most Kentucky bourbons and Tennessee whiskeys, as well as a further two minor mash bills (four-grain and non-typical) that are less common but in use among some craft distillers. Of the three major bourbon bills, the rye mash bill is the most commonly used and consists of about 75–80% corn, 10–15% rye and 5–10% malted barley. As you might expect, the high-rye mash bill increases the rye content, shifting the balance to about 55–77% corn, 18–35% rye and 5–10% malted barley. The wheated mash bill replaces rye entirely and instead uses wheat, commonly at a ratio of about 70–81% corn, 14–20% wheat and 5–10% malted barley. The two lesser-used mash bills offer a little more flexibility for craft distillers to experiment with. The four-grain mash bill is a combination of corn, rye, wheat and malted barley, but since this is less common it is difficult to give approximate ratios. Lastly, the non-typical mash bill refers to any mash that includes secondary grains other than rye or wheat. Some distillers have included oats, millet, quinoa, triticale, spelt and even brown rice in their bourbon mashes. Each of these grains adds unique flavours and characteristics to the mouthfeel of the final product.

fermentation process. Water with the right pH will also help the yeast outcompete other microorganisms that might otherwise spoil the mash.

Skipping ahead briefly, good water plays an important role in proofing the spirit down from cask (*see* page 35) to bottling strength, as water with a high mineral content can cause salts and minerals to solidify and collect on the bottom of the bottle. Alternatively, water with almost no mineral content affects the aroma and mouthfeel of the spirit. So the right type of water is very important.

Bourbon is Born

Cooking

Once a mash bill has been selected, the grains are milled, mixed with water and cooked, breaking down the proteins in the grains and gelatinizing the starch. After the starch is gelatinized, the enzymes in the malted barley begin to break down the starch molecules in the mash bill into fermentable sugars. The process to this point is similar to the mashing process in beer making, and in an efficient distillery, can take as little as an hour to complete.

▼ Sour Mash Process

Next, the cooked mash is cooled down and pumped to the fermentation tank. This can vary from closed stainless steel tanks to rustic open tanks made from cypress wood, or anything in between. The mash needs to be cooled to about

Left Woodford Reserve is one of a few bourbon distilleries that use open top wooden fermentation tanks.

21°C (70°F), at which point the sour mash process takes place. Previously fermented mash (sometimes called backset) and/or spent beer – the leftover liquid from the still after all the alcohol has been stripped out – is added to a new ferment at this stage. Both backset and spent beer have a low pH and taste sour. And, as Dr Crow demonstrated (*see* page 15), lowering the pH of the new mash helps the yeast propagate quickly to outcompete other microorganisms, giving higher yields.

▼ Distillation

Distillation is the process of separating various chemical compounds based on boiling points. Because alcohol boils at 78.4°C (173°F) and water boils at 100°C (212°F), slowly heating a mixture will cause the alcohol to evaporate first, leaving behind most of the water. This simple idea has been practiced for millenia around the world. However, it wasn't until the 8th century AD that the scientist Abu Mūsā Jābir ibn Hayyān, sometimes referred to as "the father of chemistry", made a major technological advance in distilling with the creation of the alembic pot still. This was so effective that pot stills based on this design are still being used.

The last major advancement in distilling technology

Right The Persian Abu Mūsā Jābir ibn Hayyān (721–815), also known as Geber, was a prominent alchemist, and all-around scientist who helped perfect the alembic still.

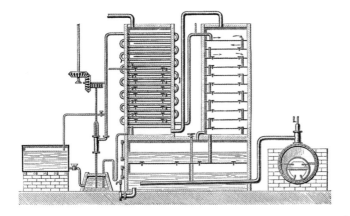

occurred in 1830 when Aeneas Coffey, an Irish excise tax collector, was granted a patent for two column stills in series that could be operated continuously. The Coffey still, as it became known, was highly efficient, could produce spirits that were much cleaner and smoother than those made in other stills of its time and could be fed non-stop. Coffey's design ideas for the continuous column still became so popular they remain in use today and are used to make most bourbon, Canadian whisky and Scottish grain whisky.

Above The 19th-century Coffey still, patented by the Irishman Aeneas Coffey, was one of the last major advances in distillation technology.

Below One section of the column still at Angel's Envy Distillery, in Louisville, Kentucky.

At almost all large Kentucky bourbon distilleries, fully fermented mash – sometimes referred to as distiller's beer – is pumped from the fermentation tank to the beer still (a very large column filled with perforated plates). The beer, grist and all, is pumped in near the top of the still while large amounts of steam are pumped in from the bottom. As the beer and steam meet, the heat causes the alcohol and other volatile compounds to boil and rise toward the top of the still. As these vapours rise, they recondense on perforated plates inside the still and revaporize as they are hit with more steam. This process of boiling, condensing and reboiling is repeated again and again throughout the entire height of the still, causing alcohol vapours to concentrate at the top while the majority of the water and all of the solids fall to the bottom, to be pumped out as spent beer.

After leaving the beer still, the alcohol vapours pass through a second vessel known as a doubler. The doubler is filled with an alcohol solution called "low wines", which is usually somewhere in the 30% ABV range. As the alcohol vapours pass through the doubler it further concentrates the alcohol, and the resulting distillate – sometimes referred to as "white dog" – comes off the still at about 69–70% ABV.

Above Craft distilleries have proliferated across the US from three or four in the mid-1980s to more than 1,300 in 2017.

In addition to alcohol and flavour compounds, there are a number of potentially harmful compounds which must be removed from the distillate. Acetone, methanol, butanol and more – all of which are a natural part of the organic chemistry that occurs during fermentation – are known to be dangerous in concentrated amounts. The distiller, therefore, must take great care to separate out as much of these potentially harmful compounds as possible, while collecting the majority of the alcohol and the flavour and aromatic compounds that give the drink its pleasant taste.

In a modern column still, the processes of feeding the still, concentrating the alcohol, separating out the harmful compounds and removing the spent beer all happen simultaneously. However, in a pot still, which is more commonly used among craft distillers, each of these steps is more distinct and easily observed. Since pot stills are less efficient, it typically takes two runs to make a single batch of distillate that will go into a barrel.

▼ The Stripping Run

The aim of the first run, called the stripping run, is to simply concentrate the alcohol as much as possible from the solids and some of the water. The still is "charged" with beer and the distiller begins heating the still, either by using a steam jacket around the outside of the still or an old-fashioned direct flame. Either way, the contents of the still need to be stirred constantly to prevent any of the solids from burning and tainting the batch with unpleasant flavours. During the stripping run, the low wines that come off the still are collected and saved for the second spirit run.

▼ The Spirit Run

During the spirit run the distiller has to make some very important choices on when to make his or her cuts. As the still heats up to about 56°C (132.8°F), acetone begins to boil and vaporize, followed by methanol at 64.7°C (148.5°F). As these vapours rise to the top of the pot they come to a junction called the lyne arm, which connects the pot to the condenser. Once the vapours enter the condenser, a cold liquid circulates around the pipe carrying them. As the vapours cool, they recondense and come out of the still as a liquid. Since this first liquid off the still, called the "heads", contains a variety of hazardous chemicals, it is collected in a special container and is either discarded or occasionally used to clean the floors. After the heads have been "cut", and the distiller notices that the unpleasant solvent notes have disappeared, what's known as the "hearts" will start to be collected. Made up of pleasant flavour and aromatic compounds, alcohol and some heavier fusel alcohols – this will eventually become the bourbon you find in the bottle.

As the hearts cut nears its end, the spirit coming from the still will taste very hot and harsh, even though the alcohol content is decreasing. When making a white spirit, such as vodka, gin, unaged brandy or rum, the aim is to cut out all of the fusel alcohols because they are unpleasant to drink. However, when producing a spirit to age, the distiller wants to leave some amount of fusel alcohols in the hearts cut because they will eventually oxidize and add more character and complexity to the spirit over time. Once the flavour shifts away from the pleasant characteristics the distiller is looking for, the hearts will stop being collected and the "tails" cut will be made. The tails consist of ethanol, fusel alcohols and a number of heavier aroma and flavour compounds that are typically unpleasant. Some distillers turn the still off at this point, while others keep it running and recycle some of the tails into the next stripping run to get a little extra alcohol out of the next batch.

Above Top of the copper column stills inside Maker's Mark Distillery.

Ageing and Barrelling

Ultimately, when making bourbon, a recipe is not crafted for what it will taste like coming off the still, but rather how it will taste coming out of the barrel. It takes a little imagination and a lot of practical experience not to distil for today but for four, six, eight, even twenty years in the future.

Unlike the laws for Scotch whisky, which require both a minimum number of years in wood and a maximum barrel size, bourbon's definition does not specify a length of time or a barrel size (*see* pages 38 and 40). However, in practice almost all bourbon is aged in 200 litre (53 gallon) barrels made from charred new American white oak (*Quercus alba*) for at least four years. It is easy to think of the maturation phase as a period of inactivity, but that would be far from the truth.

Oak

Before the barrel is made, tall oak trees from the Ozark Mountains are logged, split and cut into staves. The most prized barrels come from "yard-seasoned" staves, which have been stacked outside and left to the elements. Oak is mostly made of cellulose, which gives the wood its structural integrity and allows the barrel to be watertight – but being watertight also means the whiskey cannot interact much with the wood, which is why seasoning is so important. The heat, cold, rain, humidity and sunlight cause mould and other forms of microorganisms to grow on the wood staves as they sit for 12–36 months out in the yard. During this time the wood degrades slightly, developing

Right A factory worker assembles white oak staves into a barrel at the Brown-Forman cooperage facility in Louisville, Kentucky.

very tiny fractures, which allow the bourbon to penetrate deeper into the wood, picking up some of its characteristics and infusing the end drink with flavour.

▼ **Charring**

Once the wood is fully seasoned, it is taken to the cooper, who fashions it by hand into a barrel. The finished barrel (minus the end caps) is then placed over a small fire and the interior is allowed to burn. The resulting char creates a layer of charcoal that acts like a filter as the whiskey is pushed in and out of the wood by seasonal cycles of cold and hot temperatures. How long the fire burns determines how deeply the layer of char penetrates the barrel, and this length of time is measured in numbers: for a No. 1 char, the fire lasts for 15 seconds; No. 2 char lasts for 30 seconds; No. 3 char for 35 seconds; and the No. 4 – or alligator – char for 55 seconds. Char numbers 3 and 4 are the most commonly found, but the different timescales involved offer more adventurous distillers room to experiment. Buffalo Trace Distillery once released a handful of identical bourbons with differing levels of char, going all the way to No. 7.

▼ **Ageing**

As the bourbon sits ageing in the barrels, the flavour compounds from fermentation that have been concentrated in the still begin to interact and mix with the char and the oak compounds extracted by the alcohol. In addition to this, oxygen is able to pass through the wood and react with the spirit as the barrel sits in the warehouse. This process of oxidation slowly breaks down some of the harsher fusel alcohols into smaller components that add body and greater complexity to the end product.

Left Barrels of Woodford Reserve Kentucky Straight Bourbon Whiskey wait to be rolled down the run track to the warehouses for ageing at the company's distillery in Versailles, Kentucky.

This intricate process of maturation is complicated by the
fact that even small changes in a barrel's temperature or the
average humidity in the surrounding air can significantly
affect the flavour of the bourbon inside. Generally, barrels
that sit on the top floors of a rickhouse – a special warehouse
used to store bourbon barrels – are spicier, more intense
and have more oak flavours, whereas the barrels on the
slightly cooler, more humid lower floors have a softer
character with less intensity. Because no two barrels are
the same, producers will usually take multiple barrels, from
different parts of the rickhouse, and mix them to build the
desired flavour profile.

 Vatting

This process of mixing barrels is known as vatting, or
blending. Blending is sometimes looked down on in the
bourbon world because – according to US government
guidelines – blended whiskey is a category of spirits allowed
to contain a mixture of 20% whiskey and up to 80% "neutral
spirit" (high strength vodka). Despite this negative
association, the ability of a master blender to create a
consistent flavour profile again and again from different
barrels is a tremendous skill.

 Filtering

Once vatted, producers make the decision whether or not to
filter the bourbon. Some producers choose not to filter their
bourbon because they believe it can negatively affect its
flavour. Others may charcoal filter – a process that primarily
removes any small residual particulate from the barrel and
polishes the look of the spirit (*see also* page 41) – or chill

filter their bourbon. Chill filtering is a process in which the whiskey is quickly cooled to between -10°C (14°F) and 4°C (39°F) and then pushed through a filter. Chilling the whiskey causes fatty acid chains to make the spirit cloudy. As the bourbon is filtered, the fatty acids are removed, producing a clearer liquid. The fatty acids are not necessarily harmful, but some producers choose to protect the visual appeal of the bourbon especially in areas with very cold winters. Some critics of chill filtration believe that these fatty acids positively contribute to the flavour and body of the whiskey and that keeping them is worth any potential cloudiness.

▼ Proofing

Finally, the last step in the process before bottling is to reduce the alcohol content of the bourbon from cask strength (*see* page 41) to bottling strength. If the bourbon is at 62% ABV after being vatted and filtered, and the target strength is 45% ABV, pure water is gradually added to the bourbon until the target strength is reached. This needs to be done slowly, because if water is added too quickly it can cause a chemical reaction which gives the spirit a faint aroma of liquid soap. Once the water is added, the bourbon is allowed to rest so that the alcohol and water fully integrate.

When rested, the bourbon is ready to be bottled, labelled and shipped, ultimately to be opened and enjoyed at your local bar or at home.

Left Bourbon and American whiskey have been at the forefront of the craft cocktail boom, which has helped bourbon exceed vodka in value sold in the US for the first time since the 1970s.

3

When you pick up a bottle of bourbon, the label provides a lot of information about the liquid contained inside – especially if you know what to look for. This information can be traced back to the very first consumer protection legislation passed by the US Congress in 1897 – the Bottled-in-Bond Act. The Act served as the basis from which all other US alcohol labelling laws sprung and these laws help to inform consumers about what they are buying simply by reading the label. *See* pages 37–43 for a rough guide of the information usually included.

HOW TO READ A BOURBON LABEL

Now, it is also true that the label may not tell you everything you want to know, or in some cases may be slightly misleading – which is why it is important to know how to read a bourbon label and understand what is and what is not being said. The following guide will define some of the basic bourbon terms found on labels and allow you to understand exactly what you are looking at. Many are legally defined by the US government and as such are part of the DNA of any bourbon, while some are just marketing-speak designed to lure in the uninformed.

Age Statements

By US law, bourbon is required to have an age statement for the youngest bourbon in the bottle on the front, back, side or neck label. However, there is an exception to this rule. If a bourbon is labelled as straight or bottled-in-bond and is aged for at least four years, the producer has the option of not adding an additional age statement on the label. This is why there are no specific age statements listed on Jim Beam White Label, Evan Williams Black Label, Wild Turkey 101 and many other straight bourbons from Kentucky. One recent trend seen mostly on craft bourbons and bourbons from non-distilling producers (NDPs) has been the use of "Aged less than 4 years". Labels featuring this are an unfortunate development, because they do not conform to either the letter or the spirit of the law. The purpose of requiring an age statement is to allow consumers to make an informed decision when making their purchase. Saying something is less than four years old isn't as clear as it could be – is it six months old? Or three years? Producers who use this statement on their labels might be making fine bourbon, but they are not being completely transparent.

Brand Name

An obvious inclusion, you will probably find this on the bottle in some shape or form. The brand name is also sometimes known as the fanciful name.

State of Distillation

It is required by US law that all bourbon bottles specify the state in which the whiskey was distilled, and this information can be found in a few places on the bottle. It is usually specified quite clearly on the front, but some bourbon producers – particularly those outside of Kentucky – choose instead to put the state of distillation on the back. Taking Jim Beam as an example, you'll see the state once on the front label identifying that the straight bourbon is from the state of Kentucky and again on the back label, with an address. If the bourbon is distilled in one state and bottled in a second state, the label must say "Distilled in..." separately from the bottling address on the label.

Straight

This is a US Alcohol and Tobacco Tax and Trade Bureau's (TTB) legally defined term and means a whiskey stored in a charred new oak container for at least two years and to which no colouring, flavouring or blending materials are added, other than water. Without this term, bourbon is allowed to have added harmless colouring, flavouring or blending materials that do not alter the class of the spirit – similar to Scotch whisky, which can have a colouring agent known as E150a added without the need for it to be specified on the label.

Blended Bourbon

"A blend" is a legally defined term, specifying whiskey that must contain at least 51% straight bourbon blended with other whiskey and/or a neutral spirit such as high-proof vodka. Blended bourbon may also contain harmless colouring, flavouring or blending materials.

Blended Straight Bourbon Whiskeys

"Blended" or "a blend of" straight bourbon whiskeys is legally defined by the TTB as a mixture of straight bourbon whiskeys that come from more than one producer in one or more states. These blends are also allowed to contain harmless colouring, flavouring or blending materials. If the mixture includes straight bourbons from two or more states then the producer is not required to put the state of distillation on the label. Most examples of blended straight bourbon whiskeys on the market today are this sort of mixture, combining bourbons from more than one state.

Sour Mash

This is an unregulated term that can refer to two different production techniques that aid in the fermentation of a bourbon mash. One method takes a portion of a fermented mash that is full of live yeast and pitches it into a new unfermented batch of grain. This inoculates the new mash with some active yeast and lowers the pH level of the mash, making it more acidic, which is good for the yeast and bad for other bacteria that could cause the mash to spoil. A second method sometimes referred to as a sour mash is when spent beer (the remaining liquid and solids left over after the alcohol has been stripped out) is added to a new batch of fermenting grain. While the spent beer does not have any live yeast, it does have a low pH level, which helps the fresh yeast in the new mash outcompete any bacteria or other microorganisms.

Whiskey

Whiskey is a general class of spirit – and, as the saying goes, all bourbons are whiskey but not all whiskeys are bourbon. The TTB defines whiskey as an alcoholic distillate made from a fermented mash of grain distilled to less than 95% alcohol by volume (ABV) in such a way that it "possesses the taste, aroma and characteristics generally attributed to whiskey", stored in oak barrels and bottled at a minimum of 40% ABV. Interestingly, even though whiskey spelt with an "e" is the most common spelling in the United States, the TTB spells whisky without an "e" in all of its rules – with "whiskey" to be used on labels as an allowable alternative spelling. What this means in practice is that most bourbon producers choose to spell whiskey with an "e", although a few brands such as Maker's Mark have adopted the spelling (without an "e") more common to the rest of the world.

Bourbon

"Bourbon" is a TTB legally defined term, meaning a whiskey made from a fermented mash of grains – with no less than 51% corn – distilled to no more than 80% ABV and stored at no more than 62.5% ABV in a charred new oak container. In addition to corn, the typical grains found in bourbon are rye, wheat and malted barley, although any grain could be included. What you might notice is absent from the definition of bourbon is a statement about where it is made and how long the bourbon must stay in the barrel. The reasons are simple. First, bourbon can be made anywhere in the United States, not just Kentucky. Second, there is no legally mandated length of time a bourbon must stay in the charred new oak barrel unless it is modified with the term straight or bottled-in-bond. This means a bourbon could be stored in the barrel for as long as it takes to fill it up and then immediately be dumped. In practice, of course, almost no one does this and the vast majority of bourbon consumed around the world is at least four years old.

Tennessee Whiskey

Since the signing of the North American Free Trade Agreement in 1992, all US trade agreements have included protection for Tennessee whiskey as a straight bourbon whiskey distinctive to the State of Tennessee. In May 2013, Tennessee went a step further and created a state law that officially defined Tennessee whiskey as: a spirit manufactured in Tennessee; filtered through maple charcoal prior to ageing, also known as the Lincoln County Process; made from grain that consists of at least 51% corn; distilled to no more than 160 proof (80% ABV); aged in charred new oak barrels; placed in the barrel at no more than 125 proof (62.5% ABV); and bottled at not less than 80 proof (40% ABV). The last five parts of this definition exactly mirror the TTB's legal definition for bourbon, which means Tennessee whiskey is bourbon, but most Tennessee whiskey producers choose not to label it as bourbon – presumably for marketing reasons.

Small Batch

"Small batch" is an unregulated term invented by Kentucky bourbon distillers to distinguish certain bourbons in their portfolio from the rest. As the term is not legally outlined there is no singular definition. Generally, it has come to mean that the bourbon in the bottle comes from a small number of barrels (often 50–200), compared to the thousands of barrels used for a single bottling run of a large brand. It is claimed that this smaller number allows the producer to be more discerning. That being said, "small batch" is pure marketing-speak and is almost impossible to quantify in terms of actual value for the consumer. Despite this vagueness, the term has caught on since Heaven Hill first released its Elijah Craig Small Batch Bourbon in 1986, and countless producers both big and small have used it as a justification for a higher price point.

Single Barrel

"Single barrel" is another term that is not legally defined by the TTB – however, it does require all labels to be truthful, so the plain meaning of the term is self-evident and refers to the fact that all of the whiskey in the bottle came from one barrel. It is common on single barrel bourbon labels to see the producer list the barrel number that the bottle was filled from.

Bottled-in-Bond

This is a legally defined term for a whiskey that has been aged for at least four years in charred new oak containers, the product of one single distillery, from one single distilling season and bottled at exactly 100 proof (50% ABV). This was once the gold standard for bourbon and a true sign of quality, but bottled-in-bond bourbons slowly fell out of favour as bourbon producers chased the changing tastes of drinkers in the 1970s and 1980s toward lighter flavoured spirits. However, both the large Kentucky distilleries and a growing number of craft distillers are offering bottled-in-bond bourbon once again as a product of quality and authenticity.

Craft

The word craft when it comes to distilled spirits is a completely unregulated term by the TTB. However, there are a few organizations that have created definitions to help bring clarity. The most universally accepted aspect of what defines a craft distillery or a craft spirit is production size. While this can range from 30,000–750,000 proof gallons, depending on the organization, the main idea is that craft spirits come from distilleries that have significantly smaller total capacity compared to Jim Beam, for example, which in 2016 sold about 9 million proof gallons. A proof gallon is 1 gallon of spirit at 50% ABV. The American Distilling Institute and the American Craft Spirits Association both add an additional condition that craft spirits come from distilleries which are independently owned, not owned by a conglomerate of spirit brands or a multinational corporation. Well aware of the large market share big beer brands have lost to craft brewers, large spirit brands have begun incorporating the craft language into their marketing materials in an attempt to cash in on the interest in craft spirits and slow any potential loss of market share.

Alcohol Concentration

US law requires all bourbons to disclose the concentration of alcohol in the spirit by volume, expressed as a percentage. Many bourbons are around the 40% ABV mark, which is the lowest legally allowable ABV for a bourbon to be bottled at in the United States. However, outside the US it is possible to find examples of bourbon bottled at less than 40% ABV. The TTB also allows producers the option to include the alcohol concentration expressed in US proof, which is simply two times the ABV – so a 40% ABV bourbon is 80 proof.

Cask Strength/Barrel Proof

"Cask strength" and "barrel proof" are not legally defined terms, but they refer to the fact that the bourbon in the bottle has not been diluted with water to reduce its strength (*see* page 35). This does not mean that the bourbon has not been filtered. It is still possible that the spirit was lightly filtered to remove any charcoal sediment from the barrel or it was chill filtered to remove excess fatty acids that can cause a spirit to become cloudy.

Non Chill Filtered

Chill filtering is a process by which bourbon is cooled down to a temperature between -10°C (14°F) and 4°C (39°F), then filtered through paper to remove any long-chain fatty acids (*see also* page 35). These fatty acids are not dangerous in any way but they can cause a spirit to look cloudy and less attractive, so this is done mostly for aesthetic reasons. However, some producers claim that these fatty acids contribute to the flavour and mouthfeel of the spirit, so will proudly state that their bourbons are not chill filtered.

Charcoal Filtered

Charcoal filtration is a process in which the bourbon passes through a charcoal medium to remove any sediment from the barrel or larger particles (the process is not dissimilar to charcoal filters that many people use to filter drinking water). There is no requirement for this filtration to take place, but it generally occurs after the matured barrels have been dumped and before the bourbon is proofed down. It has been incorrectly claimed by some that the reason Tennessee whiskey (*see* page 39) is not labelled as bourbon is because it goes through what is known as the Lincoln County Process, in which the new spirit is charcoal filtered before going into a barrel. Charcoal filtration does not prohibit a company in any way from labelling its whiskey as a bourbon.

1 — YEARS **8** OLD

2 — OLD **BOURBON**

KENTUCKY

3 — STRAIGHT BOURBON WHISKEY — **5**

BOTTLED-IN-BOND — **6**

4 — SOUR MASH

9 — FINISHED BOURBON

50% Alc/Vol | 100 PROOF — **7**

Charcoal Filtered — **8**

Finished Bourbon

Finished bourbon describes a process where the whiskey is dumped from its original charred new oak barrel and transferred to a second barrel that previously contained another liquid, such as beer, wine, sherry, port, rum, brandy, maple syrup or even roasted coffee beans. This second maturation is usually over a much shorter period, but allows the bourbon to pick up additional flavours before it is vatted, proofed and bottled. Maker's 46 (see page 130) is made using an interesting process whereby Maker's Mark adds toasted French oak staves to its own barrels and reseals them for an additional year or so, which the company claims adds an extra spice character to the bourbon.

Address for Production

It is a requirement of US law to include the state in which the whiskey was distilled and bottled. The industry norm is just to list the city and state but there are loopholes in this process that can actually obscure where and who made the bourbon in the bottle. Producers are permitted to use a different business name, also known as a DBA (Doing Business As), meaning a larger company can subcontract a distillery to create its bourbon and hide the name of either from the bottle – giving an impression of a more local, small-scale production. This is not to say that the bourbon within is bad, but this marketing sleight of hand means that you need to take this information with a pinch of salt.

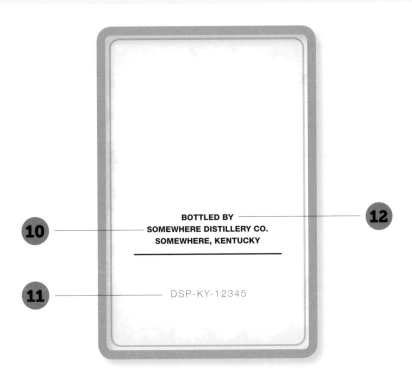

DSP Number

A Distilled Spirits Producer (DSP) number is assigned to a facility when it receives its US federal permit to operate a distillery, or some other business that handles or bottles distilled spirits, and includes the state along with a specific number. For example, Jim Beam operates DSP-KY-230, which is a distillery in Clermont, Kentucky, and California's Sonoma County Distilling Company operates its distillery out of DSP-CA-15097. At present, including the DSP number on a label is completely optional, although some have suggested that if this became mandatory it could help consumers to make informed decisions about their purchases and provide greater transparency.

Production Statements

TTB requires all bourbon labels to say "Bottled by" followed by the company that put the bourbon into the bottle. This can be modified to: "Produced and bottled by", "Made by", "Handmade", "Crafted" and "Handcrafted" etc. None of these, however, necessarily mean that the company actually fermented, distilled, aged and bottled the bourbon, only that the company took bourbon barrels and bottled the contents. If you are interested in drinking whiskey actually made by a particular distillery, look for the words "Distilled and bottled by" – some have gone a step further to include "Fermented, distilled, aged and bottled by" on the label.

SMALL BATCH

1792

KENTUCKY STRAIGHT BOURBON WHISKEY
46.85% ALC / VOL (93.7 PROOF)

BUFFALO TRACE

KENTUCKY
STRAIGHT BOURBON
WHISKEY

ELIJAH CRAIG®

SINGLE BARREL

Aged **23** *Years*

KENTUCKY
STRAIGHT BOURBON
WHISKEY

45% ALC/VOL

JACK DANIEL'S

Old Time Distillery®

OLD TIME | Nº7 BRAND | SOUR MASH

QUALITY

Tennessee WHISKEY

DISTILLED AND BOTTLED BY
JACK DANIEL DISTILLERY,
LEM MOTLOW, PROPRIETOR

JIM BEAM®

SIGNATURE CRAFT

James B Beam

| SMALL BATCH | KENTUCKY STRAIGHT BOURBON WHISKEY. aged for: **12 YEARS** | **86** PROOF | 750 mL OF KENTUCKY'S FINEST | SMALL BATCH |
| | | **43%** ALC/VOL | | |

· COPPER STILL · TRIPLE DISTILLATION ·

JOHN J. BOWMA

⟶ PIONEER SPIRIT ⟶

VIRGINIA
STRAIGHT BOURBON
WHISKEY

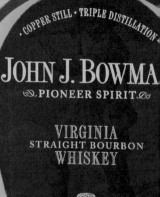

SINGLE  BARREL

OLD FORESTER®

ESTD 1870

1897

KENTUCKY STRAIGHT BOURBON WHISKY

With the passage of the Bottled in Bond Act of
1897, Old Forester transitioned from 90 proof to
100 proof. Originally produced on Louisville's
Whiskey Row, this whiskey has a rich, bold
character reminiscent of a 19th-century bourbon.

750mL 50% ALCOHOL BY VOLUME (100 PROOF)
10029482

Waitsburg Bourbon

WHISKEY

Batch Nº	Case Nº	Distiller:
ALC/VOL. 12	PROOF 1	VOL.750mL
60	120	

OOLA

CASK STRENGTH

WYOMING

44% ALC/VOL

WW

88 PROOF

WHISKEY

SMALL BATCH BOURBON WHISKE

DISTILLED, BARRELED & BOTTLED IN KIRBY, WYOMING

WYOMING

PART 2

THE BOURBONS

Neat

Water

Rocks

Cocktail

DRINKING RECOMMENDATION KEY

There is no wrong way to drink bourbon or incorrect vessel to drink bourbon from. That being said, if you want to practise noticing the aromas and flavours in your bourbon, a standard Glencairn whisky glass will do the job quite nicely. The shape helps to concentrate the aromas of the whiskey just above the rim of the glass where your nose is. Unlike nosing wine, bourbon has a higher ABV so it is not necessary to stick your nose into the glass.

THE BOURBON PROFILES

Price Range

$ less than $20

$$ $20–49

$$$ $50–79

$$$$ $80–119

$$$$$ $120 or more

Price ranges are given as approximate US retail prices at the time of publication. These will vary by location due to local taxes. Ranges are intended as a general sense of where the whiskey falls in the spectrum from a value bourbon to a super ultra-premium bourbon.

BOURBON PROFILE KEY

Strength

This is shown as ABV (Alcohol by Volume) and US proof (2x ABV). The proof of some bottlings of bourbon may vary. The strength specified relates to the particular bourbon described in the Flavour profile.

Age Statement

This refers to the youngest whiskey in the bottle, although it can contain older whiskeys.

NAS (No Age Statement) – US law requires the youngest bourbon in the bottle to be at least four years old.

Mash Bill

Rye mash: corn, rye (18% or less), malted barley
High-rye mash: corn, rye (more than 18%), malted barley
Wheated mash: corn, wheat (35% or less), malted barley
Four-grain mash: corn, rye, wheat, malted barley

The Barton 1792 Distillery was founded in 1879 and is named after the year in which Kentucky became a state. With 29 barrel-ageing warehouses and its own spring, the distillery sits in 79 hectares (196 acres) of land in Bardstown, Kentucky. Originally sold under the label "Ridgewood Reserve 1792", 1792 Small Batch Bourbon was renamed in 2004 following a trademark infringement dispute with the Brown-Forman Corporation. Eventually, "Ridgewood Reserve" was removed from the label completely. The whiskey uses a high-rye recipe and is blended from a select number of barrels. The distillery has also released a series of limited edition whiskeys, including 1792 Sweet Wheat Bourbon, 1792 High Rye Bourbon and 1792 Port Finish, in addition to 1792 Single Barrel Bourbon and a Full Proof expression.

1792 Small Batch Kentucky Straight Bourbon Whiskey

FLAVOUR This bourbon has charred wood on the nose, with a bright, tart note of grape. After a second or two, there is a flash of floral rose and vanilla blossom and a dash of lemon curd, among more classic oak notes. On the palate, good standard wood notes stand out: bright vanilla and an array of floral notes. The finish is of clean, vibrant oak with a dash of blossom and apricot jam. This is a surprisingly floral bourbon that would work beautifully in a Bourbon Sidecar or with lots of ice and a dash of Cointreau.

STRENGTH
41.9% ABV
(83.8 proof)

MASH BILL
High-rye mash

STILL TYPE
Column still

AGE STATEMENT
NAS

DISTILLERY
Barton 1792 Distillery,
Bardstown, Kentucky

BRAND OWNER
Sazerac

PRICE RANGE
$$

DRINKING RECOMMENDATION

Founded by Al Laws in 2006, Laws Whiskey House began making whiskey in 2011 and released its first batch in 2014. Laws prides itself on using the finest ingredients. It sources its wheat, rye and malted barley from a local malt house in Colorado and its corn comes from Wisconsin. Its four-grain mash bill is fermented in open-air vessels before being pot distilled and barrelled in charred new oak. Because of the altitude and the weather, maturing spirits in Colorado has a slightly different effect on the whiskey than, say, in Kentucky. After the bourbon has matured, it is vatted and brought down to 95 proof.

A.D. Laws Four Grain Straight Bourbon Whiskey

STRENGTH
47.5% ABV (95 proof)

MASH BILL
60% corn, 20% wheat, 10% rye, 10% malted barley

STILL TYPE
Pot still

AGE STATEMENT
2 years

DISTILLERY
Laws Whiskey House, Denver, Colorado

BRAND OWNER
Laws Whiskey House

PRICE RANGE
$$$

FLAVOUR The nose is very light and bready, with notes of caramel, malt, unfiltered (cloudy) apple juice and black pepper. At first sip, grain flavours explode on your tongue, followed by sweet notes of caramel and then dry oak. The finish is long, smooth and has a semisweet character that tastes of apples and yeasty bread. While this is not a traditional profile, it is a light, grain-forward bourbon that is rich in character. It is a fascinating bourbon that might appeal to fans of malt or blended malt whiskeys. Drink it neat or use it to make an excellent tall cocktail like a Highball.

DRINKING RECOMMENDATION

In addition to its two-year-old straight bourbon (*see* page 48), Laws Whiskey House also produces a four-grain bottled-in-bond bourbon. This is made in the same way as its regular straight bourbon; however, the bottled-in-bond is aged for a minimum of four years and all of the whiskey in the bottle is made in one distilling season at Laws. Once the barrels have reached maturity, they are vatted and the bourbon is reduced in strength with only water to 100 proof.

A.D. Laws Four Grain Straight Bourbon Whiskey Bottled-in-Bond

FLAVOUR The nose is light and aromatic with notes of yeast, pear cider and cedar wood. On the palate the bourbon is big, with a sweet full-bodied mouthfeel paired with light fruit and floral notes. The finish is warm and dry on the tongue, of medium length with lingering notes of apple, spice and oak. This is another unique bourbon with a non-traditional flavour profile – it's good to know this going in, not because it is bad but because it may be unexpected. The Laws bourbons demonstrate that there is a wide range of flavour profiles for bourbon yet to tap.

STRENGTH
50% ABV (100 proof)

MASH BILL
60% corn, 20% wheat, 10% rye, 10% malted barley

STILL TYPE
Pot still

AGE STATEMENT
4 years

DISTILLERY
Laws Whiskey House, Denver, Colorado

BRAND OWNER
Laws Whiskey House

PRICE RANGE
$$$

DRINKING RECOMMENDATION

Ancient Age Bourbon was first released in 1946. The brand and the Albert B. Blanton Distillery were bought in the whiskey downturn of the 1980s by Ferdie Falk and Bob Baranaskas, two former executives for Fleischmann's Distilling. Re-named Age International, it sold largely to the growing Japanese market until 1992 when the new Japanese owner sold the distillery to Sazerac, who renamed it Buffalo Trace. The now Japanese Age International kept the brands and corporate identity however, and as a result, Age International and Sazerac have a very close relationship. All Age International bourbons are made by Sazerac with the Buffalo Trace mash bill #2. Ancient Age Bourbon is a three-year-old value bourbon bottled at 80 proof. There is also an Ancient Ancient Age 10 Star bottled at 90 proof.

Ancient Age Kentucky Straight Bourbon Whiskey

STRENGTH
40% ABV (80 proof)

MASH BILL
Buffalo Trace mash bill #2
(12–15% rye)

STILL TYPE
Column still

AGE STATEMENT
3 years

DISTILLERY
Buffalo Trace Distillery
Frankfort, Kentucky

BRAND OWNER
Age International

PRICE RANGE
$

FLAVOUR The aroma greets you with light and bright fruity plums and cherries, followed by fresh cornbread. While there is significant alcohol on the nose there is also a pleasant note of caramel lingering underneath. On the palate, the bourbon takes a turn with a bright hot note of cinnamon, tempered with oak and vanilla. The finish is hot, short and tastes lightly of caramel with some oak tannins, which leave a dry sensation in your mouth. Overall, Ancient Age is a young, hot and inexpensive bourbon whose flavours are fairly well balanced – it is probably best used in tall cocktails.

DRINKING RECOMMENDATION

Angel's Envy was founded by Master Distiller and legendary bourbon man, Lincoln Henderson. Lincoln served four decades as Master Distiller for Brown-Forman and helped to create Woodford Reserve, Gentleman Jack and Jack Daniel's Single Barrel (*see* pages 184, 107 and 108). He dreamed of taking mature bourbon and finishing it in port casks and came out of retirement to start Angel's Envy with his son Wes and grandson Kyle. They purchased six-year-old rye bourbon and finished it in 227 litre (60 gallon) ruby port casks. Lincoln passed away, aged 75, in 2013 and Wes and Kyle are continuing the work he began. In 2015, Angel's Envy was purchased by Bacardi. They also produce a cask-strength bourbon as well as a rye whiskey and a cask-strength rye finished in rum barrels.

Angel's Envy Kentucky Straight Bourbon Whiskey Finished in Port Wine Barrels

FLAVOUR The bourbon has a sweet nose of cherries and oak, with a light note of vanilla, demerara sugar and fresh plum. Once you take a sip, the whiskey starts sweet and is well balanced by oak in the mid-palate, with notes of baked apple and nutmeg. Although the whiskey is warm in the mouth, there is zero harshness. After swallowing, a pleasant warmth lingers with notes of apple and oak that are dry and have slight astringency. Overall, this is an enjoyable, light bourbon that is well balanced between oak and sweetness. This would work nicely neat, on the rocks and in a cocktail where you want a sweeter bourbon.

STRENGTH
43.3% ABV (86.6 proof)

MASH BILL
72% corn, 18% rye, 10% malted barley

STILL TYPE
Column still

AGE STATEMENT
NAS

DISTILLERY
Undisclosed Kentucky distillery

BRAND OWNER
Bacardi Limited

PRICE RANGE
$$

DRINKING RECOMMENDATION

Part of the Jim Beam Small Batch Collection (*see also* pages 53 and 127), Baker's Bourbon is named after Baker Beam, the grandnephew of Jim Beam. Baker started working at the company in 1954 and over 20 years worked his way up from the labour pool to the distiller at the Jim Beam plant in Clermont, Kentucky. The eponymous bourbon reflects Baker's personal preference for what he describes as a "robust, medium-bodied bourbon, with a silky-smooth finish". Baker's Bourbon was first released in 1992; each bottling run pulls from barrels that are at least seven years old and the whiskey is proofed down to 53.5% ABV.

Baker's Kentucky Straight Bourbon Whiskey

STRENGTH
53.5% ABV (107 proof)

MASH BILL
75% corn, 13% rye, 12% malted barley

STILL TYPE
Column still

AGE STATEMENT
7 years

DISTILLERIES
Jim Beam Distilleries, Clermont, Boston and Frankfort, Kentucky

BRAND OWNER
Beam Suntory

PRICE RANGE
$$$

FLAVOUR Rich vanilla bursts from the nose with pleasant fruity notes reminiscent of apple, cherries and orange blossom. These brighter fruit notes are nicely supported by barrel aromas of seasoned and burnt oak. On the palate the bourbon is smooth, sweet and rich, like dark cherries with a little touch of mixed spice. At the back of the palate the bourbon is dry but there is the perception of sweet molasses and dark maple syrup. On the finish the whiskey is warm, although this is not unexpected at this strength, and has a long finish of deep flavours like dried fruit, tobacco and leather. This is a really excellent high-proof bourbon with lots of flavour. Drink it neat or with a couple of drops of water to soften its edge.

DRINKING RECOMMENDATION

Basil Hayden was one of many Catholics who left the state of Maryland after the American Revolution and settled in Kentucky to escape persecution. While Basil was probably a farmer-distiller like many of his contemporaries, there is no historical record of what he might have distilled. In the late 19th century, Basil's grandson opened the Old Grand-Dad Distillery, named in Basil's honour, and produced Old Grand-Dad Bourbon, a brand that eventually ended up with the James B. Beam Distilling Company (*see* pages 142–3). In 1992, Beam debuted Basil Hayden's Bourbon as an eight-year-old Kentucky straight bourbon that uses the same high-rye mash bill as Old Grand-Dad. Today, it is a NAS Kentucky straight bourbon bottled at 40% ABV.

Basil Hayden's Kentucky Straight Bourbon Whiskey

FLAVOUR The bourbon is sweet and subtle on the nose, but fresh with bright notes of oak and a hint of creamy milk chocolate. Intermingled throughout are notes of vanilla and woody spice. It is very smooth at the start of the palate, but this nonetheless has some real power behind it. It starts out slightly sweet, with light, vibrant woody notes and just the faintest hint of fresh mint, somewhat reminiscent of a Mint Julep. It then develops on the palate, becoming warmer with peppered notes, before the initial sweetness is transformed into a rich, dry woodiness and warm spiciness on the finish. A smooth, but substantial bourbon that is great on the rocks or in short, intense cocktails like the Sazerac.

STRENGTH
40% ABV (80 proof)

MASH BILL
63% corn, 27% rye, 10% malted barley

STILL TYPE
Column still

AGE STATEMENT
NAS

DISTILLERIES
Jim Beam Distilleries, Clermont, Boston and Frankfort, Kentucky

BRAND OWNER
Beam Suntory

PRICE RANGE
$$

DRINKING RECOMMENDATION

New Holland Artisan Spirits was founded in 2005 by Brett VanderKamp and Jason Spaulding nine years after the successful launch of New Holland Brewing Company. When Beer Barrel Bourbon was first released in about 2013, New Holland was sourcing bourbon and using the barrels to age its Dragon's Milk Stout; it then put the bourbon back into the second-fill beer barrels to age for an additional three months. As a result of its finishing in a beer barrel, the bourbon picks up subtle hints from the beer that add more complexity to the spirit.

Beer Barrel Bourbon

STRENGTH
40% ABV (80 proof)

MASH BILL
70% corn, 5% rye, 25% barley

STILL TYPE
Column and pot stills

AGE STATEMENT
NAS

DISTILLERIES
New Holland Artisan Spirits, Holland, Michigan; other undisclosed distillery

BRAND OWNER
New Holland Artisan Spirits

PRICE RANGE
$$

FLAVOUR The nose is bright and inviting, with notes of vanilla, caramel and nectarine, and a light and high vegetal note from the hops, which is pleasant and well integrated. On the palate the bourbon is sweet and full-bodied with light flavours of vanilla and stone fruit. The finish is light and smooth, with a touch of sweetness and notes of green apple and spearmint. This is a very good example of how to integrate hops into a whiskey. Hopped whiskeys distilled from beer are often bitter and astringent; however, ageing this bourbon in a used beer barrel gives the bourbon a bright almost herbal character that plays well with the sweet fruit notes. The almost herbal character of the bourbon would be interesting with vermouth in cocktails. That said, you can also drink it neat and it will most likely appeal to those who enjoy sweeter bourbons and ales.

DRINKING RECOMMENDATION

Belle Meade Bourbon was first released around 1878 in a partnership between Nelson's Green Brier Distillery founded by Charles Nelson, a German-born immigrant to the United States, and Sperry Wade & Company, owners of the well-known horse farm Belle Meade Plantation. Charles and his wife Louisa ran a successful distillery selling some 30 brands of bourbon and Tennessee whiskey until State Prohibition shut them down in 1909. One hundred years later, great-great-great grandsons Andy and Charlie Nelson re-established Nelson's Green Brier Distillery and re-released Belle Meade Bourbon as a sourced whiskey made with six- to eight-year-old high-rye Indiana bourbon.

Belle Meade Sour Mash Straight Bourbon Whiskey

FLAVOUR This bourbon has a sweet nose of caramel and vanilla, followed by fruit notes of red cherries and red apple. The sweetness continues on the palate with flavours of vanilla and caramel nicely balanced with cinnamon and dry oak tannins. The finish, not surprisingly, is sweet, soft and long, with notes of cherries, cinnamon and oak. This is a nice big bourbon with a good balance between oak, sweetness and spice, and definitely one for those who like them on the sweet side. Drink it neat or use it to make a sweeter-style Manhattan.

STRENGTH
45.2% ABV (90.4 proof)

MASH BILL
64% corn, 30% rye, 6% malted barley

STILL TYPE
Column still

AGE STATEMENT
NAS

DISTILLERY
MGP, Lawrenceburg, Indiana

BRAND OWNER
Nelson's Green Brier Distillery

PRICE RANGE
$$

DRINKING RECOMMENDATION

Using the same high-rye bourbon as the straight Belle Meade (*see* page 55), Belle Meade Single Barrel Bourbon carries a ten-year age statement and is bottled at 109.6 proof.

Belle Meade Single Barrel Bourbon

STRENGTH
54.8% ABV (109.6 proof)

MASH BILL
64% corn, 30% rye, 6% malted barley

STILL TYPE
Column still

AGE STATEMENT
10 years

DISTILLERY
MGP, Lawrenceburg, Indiana

BRAND OWNER
Nelson's Green Brier Distillery

PRICE RANGE
$$$

FLAVOUR The nose pulls you in with deep notes of dark cherries, caramel and vanilla. And, while there is a noticeable note of alcohol, it is not overbearing. Initially, the palate is hot and spicy from the alcohol and grain flavours. However, the flavour then morphs into notes of oak, tobacco, leather, sweet raisins and prunes. Not surprisingly, the finish is warm, dry and long, with pleasant notes of oak and dried dates. This is a very nice bourbon that shows great balance between the dryness of the alcohol and oak, with the sweet, dried fruit character you get from a well-aged spirit. While this is likely to appeal to many bourbon fans, it will especially appeal to those who prefer sweeter bourbon. Drink it neat, with a little water to tame the alcohol, or use it to make a sweeter bourbon cocktail.

DRINKING RECOMMENDATION

In the late 19th century, Belle Meade Bourbon was so popular that it was sold across the Atlantic Ocean in Paris, France. Perhaps partially inspired by this fact, Nelson's Green Brier has released three special bourbons that were finished in European wine and spirit casks. The first release in this series was the Belle Meade Bourbon finished in sherry casks. Nelson's took nine-year-old Indiana bourbon and rested it in fine Oloroso sherry barrels; the results speak for themselves.

Belle Meade Bourbon Sherry Cask Finish

FLAVOUR This whiskey has a great nose that blends classic bourbon notes with Oloroso sherry. It is sweet vanilla and rum and raisin, with a hint of mixed spice and oak. The palate is sweet, with notes of caramel, almond, nutmeg and a hint of vanilla. The finish is long and dry, with a characteristic nutty flavour from the Oloroso and a touch of red fruit. This is a nice bourbon that really shows off the flavours picked up during the secondary maturation in sherry barrels and could potentially be a good crossover bourbon for those who love sherry-finished Scotch whisky. Drink neat and enjoy.

STRENGTH
45.2% ABV (90.4 proof)

MASH BILL
64% corn, 30% rye, 6% malted barley

STILL TYPE
Column still

AGE STATEMENT
9 years

DISTILLERY
MGP, Lawrenceburg, Indiana

BRAND OWNER
Nelson's Green Brier Distillery

PRICE RANGE
$$$

DRINKING RECOMMENDATION

This is the second release in the Belle Meade Bourbon Cask Finish Series. For this edition, the Nelson brothers took a blend of six- to nine-year-old bourbon and let it rest in cognac barrels made of French Limousin oak that held XO ("extra-old") cognac for twelve years.

Belle Meade Bourbon Cognac Cask Finish

STRENGTH
45.2% ABV (90.4 proof)

MASH BILL
64% corn, 30% rye, 6% malted barley

STILL TYPE
Column still

AGE STATEMENT
NAS

DISTILLERY
MGP, Lawrenceburg, Indiana

BRAND OWNER
Nelson's Green Brier Distillery

PRICE RANGE
$$$

FLAVOUR The sweet nose opens up with a bright note of alcohol, followed by aromas of dried fruit, vanilla and apple skins. On the tongue the bourbon is sweet with vanilla and a touch of white pepper, cherries and oak. The finish is nice – semisweet with notes of red apple, vanilla and cinnamon. Once again, Belle Meade delivers a really excellent bourbon with bright fruit notes balanced against notes of oak and spice. Drink it neat or use it in cocktails that need a slightly sweeter bourbon.

DRINKING RECOMMENDATION

Third in the Belle Meade Bourbon Cask Finish Series, the Madeira Cask Finish again takes a blend of six- to nine-year-old bourbon and gives it a second short maturation in Malmsey Madeira barrels. Madeira is a fortified wine that is heated to mimic the conditions the wine experienced being shipped across the ocean to the New World. This unique process makes Madeira a very stable wine with an incredibly long lifespan. Malmsey Madeira is known for being a sweeter-style Madeira so the Nelsons felt that it would make an excellent finish for the high-rye bourbon they use in Belle Meade.

Belle Meade Bourbon Madeira Cask Finish

FLAVOUR The nose rushes up with a powerful note of bubble gum that, after a moment to breathe, opens with a hint of caramel, oak and pleasant fruity esters like pear cider. On the tongue the bourbon is sweet and spicy, with enjoyable notes of candied orange peel, vanilla, caramel and fresh walnuts. The finish is warm and semidry, with notes of baked apple, oak, walnuts and cinnamon. Overall, this is a really tasty and interesting bourbon. The Madeira cask adds significant complexity and flavours not usually found in straight bourbon. Definitely a bourbon for those looking for something a little unique and with more complexity. Drink it neat or with a small touch of water.

STRENGTH
45.2% ABV (90.4 proof)

MASH BILL
64% corn, 30% rye, 6% malted barley

STILL TYPE
Column still

AGE STATEMENT
NAS

DISTILLERY
MGP, Lawrenceburg, Indiana

BRAND OWNER
Nelson's Green Brier Distillery

PRICE RANGE
$$$

DRINKING RECOMMENDATION

Distilled and aged at the Buffalo Trace Distillery in Frankfort, Kentucky, this is bottled from single barrels emptied by hand. The whiskey is not blended or altered at all, other than being reduced in strength. One of the distillery's early leaders, Albert B. Blanton, used to save particular barrels from the middle of Warehouse H to produce special bottlings, thus producing the first single barrel bourbon. The Blanton's brand took the concept to market in 1984 under the guidance of Master Distiller Elmer T. Lee (*see* page 80). In addition to the original, Blanton's is also available as a number of expressions (*see* pages 62–3), which are bottled at cask strength. The distinctive Blanton's bottle has appeared in a number of modern television shows and films.

Blanton's Original Single Barrel Kentucky Straight Bourbon Whiskey

STRENGTH
46.5% ABV (93 proof)

MASH BILL
Buffalo Trace mash bill #2
(12–15% rye)

STILL TYPE
Column still

AGE STATEMENT
NAS

DISTILLERY
Buffalo Trace Distillery,
Frankfort, Kentucky

BRAND OWNER
Age International

PRICE RANGE
$$$

FLAVOUR Blanton's Original has a sweet nose of oak and fruit – tropical pineapple, plus a little lemon and blackberry – on top of notes of almond and lemon shortbread. Over time, the oak notes become more prominent, along with flavours of juicy apple and creamy marzipan. More apple notes appear on the palate and it grows more spiced as the flavour develops to notes of baked apple or apple pie, keeping its sweetness. The finish is of rich, soaked oak, more apple and dry but buttery biscuit. This is a distinctively fruity bourbon with an array of dessert-like flavours and a clean, dry finish.

DRINKING RECOMMENDATION

The Special Reserve is one of Blanton's single barrel bourbons that was designed to introduce people to the range. Like the Original (*see* page 60), it is produced at the Buffalo Trace Distillery from Warehouse H single barrels that are emptied by hand. It is also in the same distinctive round bottle with a dark green label and a stopper topped with a model of a racehorse and jockey. There are eight stoppers in total, each showing a different stage of a race.

Blanton's Special Reserve Single Barrel Kentucky Straight Bourbon Whiskey

FLAVOUR Jammy strawberry and dark cherry on the nose, it is saved from oversweetness by notes of marzipan that develop into rich oak, buttery flaky pastry and hints of brandy. The bourbon has a surprisingly dry palate of oak that grows even drier toward the finish, which is smooth, with clean oak notes accompanied by dry tannins and a hint of citrus fruitiness at the end, making this reminiscent of black tea with lemon, and a dash of cinnamon spice. This is a dry whiskey with a rich, sweet nose that would work well in short cocktails that need a little sweetness like an Old Fashioned or Manhattan.

STRENGTH
40% ABV (80 proof)

MASH BILL
Buffalo Trace mash bill #2
(12–15% rye)

STILL TYPE
Column still

AGE STATEMENT
NAS

DISTILLERY
Buffalo Trace Distillery,
Frankfort, Kentucky

BRAND OWNER
Age International

PRICE RANGE
$$$$$

DRINKING RECOMMENDATION

Blanton's Gold Edition is an expression of Blanton's Original Single Barrel Bourbon (*see* page 60), produced from single barrels from Warehouse H at the Buffalo Trace Distillery in Frankfort, Kentucky, but with a richer flavour profile and higher alcoholic strength than the original and typically slightly darker in colour. Although it shares the same distinctive bottle and stopper as the other Blanton's releases, the topper and bottle are both gold in colour.

Blanton's Gold Edition Single Barrel Kentucky Straight Bourbon Whiskey

STRENGTH
51.5% ABV (103 proof)

MASH BILL
Buffalo Trace mash bill #2
(12–15% rye)

STILL TYPE
Column still

AGE STATEMENT
NAS

DISTILLERY
Buffalo Trace Distillery,
Frankfort, Kentucky

BRAND OWNER
Age International

PRICE RANGE
$$$$$

FLAVOUR Sweet, rich toasted grain and cola nut at the start of the nose, this develops into fruitier notes of peach, apple and orange with a rich, honeyed sweetness. The palate is initially sweet, with notes of cookie, fudge, dark chocolate and orange. This develops into more traditional notes of oak and almond with a punch of peppercorns. The finish is long, with nutty notes that blend seamlessly into oak and vanilla, reminiscent of crème brûlée. The finish lingers and develops further into more fundamental wood notes, alongside hints of vanilla, fresh cream, pecan and pear Tatin. A complex and sophisticated bourbon, it works well neat or over ice.

DRINKING RECOMMENDATION

Straight from the Barrel is a series of releases under the Blanton's brand. Like Blanton's other expressions, it is produced from single barrels from Warehouse H at the Buffalo Trace Distillery in Frankfort, Kentucky, but unlike its other bourbons, the releases are bottled at cask strength, so no alterations are made to the whiskey after it leaves the barrel. As a result, the proof can vary between bottlings and each one is identified with the barrel number.

Blanton's Straight from the Barrel Kentucky Straight Bourbon Whiskey

FLAVOUR The bourbon has a rich and fruity nose, full of notes of blackcurrant and cherry, combined with the dark sweetness of black liquorice and treacle. The complexities continue with notes of baked apple, with a hint of cinnamon, almond and brown sugar caramel. To taste, even with a drop of water added, this is warming and has a thick mouthfeel. The palate is complex and textured, with notes of rich wood and dashes of liquorice, cherry, raisin and apple. The finish has notes of warm caramel and brown sugar cookies, but is nonetheless dry on the tongue. Over time, hints of rye and chocolate develop. This is a complex and multifaceted whiskey – allow yourself time to explore it, either over ice or with a splash of water.

STRENGTH
64.1% ABV (128.2 proof)

MASH BILL
Buffalo Trace mash bill #2 (12–15% rye)

STILL TYPE
Column still

AGE STATEMENT
NAS

DISTILLERY
Buffalo Trace Distillery, Frankfort, Kentucky

BRAND OWNER
Age International

PRICE RANGE
$$$$$

DRINKING RECOMMENDATION

Buffalo Trace Bourbon was first released in August 1999, shortly after Sazerac renamed the George T. Stagg Distillery the Buffalo Trace Distillery (*see* page 50). According to Sazerac, former Master Distiller Elmer T. Lee was asked to come out of retirement to help create the bourbon's profile. Buffalo Trace uses its #1 mash bill and the barrels used for the brand come from the middle floors of its rickhouses. After the bourbon reaches maturation, the barrels are vatted and the whiskey is bottled at 90 proof.

Buffalo Trace Kentucky Straight Bourbon Whiskey

STRENGTH
45% ABV (90 proof)

MASH BILL
Buffalo Trace mash bill #1
(10% or less rye)

STILL TYPE
Column still

AGE STATEMENT
NAS

DISTILLERY
Buffalo Trace Distillery,
Frankfort, Kentucky

BRAND OWNER
Sazerac

PRICE RANGE
$$

FLAVOUR While the nose on this bourbon is somewhat closed, there are clear notes of caramel and sweet, inviting notes of fresh apple with a hint of camomile. The whiskey has a medium body that starts sweet on the tongue with light notes of caramel and vanilla and then opens with flavours of oak and spice. The bourbon has a pleasant warmth and dry tannins without any harshness or astringency. The finish is semidry and medium-long, with lingering notes of oak and caramel. Buffalo Trace is a solid bourbon for both newcomers and the well initiated. It is inexpensive, flavourful and versatile. Drink it neat, on the rocks and in short or tall cocktails.

DRINKING RECOMMENDATION

Bulleit Bourbon was created in 1995 by Tom Bulleit, a lawyer from Frankfort, Kentucky. While there is no historical evidence to support Mr Bulleit's claim that his bourbon was made from a generations-old family recipe, we do know he created the brand and used sourced whiskey to sell Kentucky bourbon in the Japanese market. In 1997, Seagram purchased Bulleit Bourbon with Bulleit and family remaining as brand ambassadors. In 2000 Diageo purchased the Bulleit brand and began contracting with the Four Roses Distillery to supply the whiskey for Bulleit Bourbon. This contract expired in 2013 and it is unclear if it continues to buy bourbon but, in response to the brand's growing needs, Diageo opened a new Bulleit Distillery in Shelbyville, Kentucky, equipped with a 107cm (42 inch) diameter column still.

Bulleit Bourbon Kentucky Straight Bourbon Whiskey

FLAVOUR The first thing you notice on the nose is a sharp note of alcohol followed by sweet cherries, mixed spice and vanilla. The palate is smooth and full-bodied, with notes of caramel, cinnamon, milk chocolate and oak. The finish is bright and slightly sweet with notes of fresh apple, followed by oak and rye grain. There is also a rich and dark flavour reminiscent of milk chocolate. This is a nice bourbon that is well balanced and can be drunk neat, on the rocks or in a cocktail.

STRENGTH
45% ABV (90 proof)

MASH BILL
68% corn, 28% rye, 4% malted barley

STILL TYPE
Column still

AGE STATEMENT
NAS

DISTILLERIES
Four Roses Distillery, Lawrenceburg, Kentucky; other undisclosed Kentucky distillery

BRAND OWNER
Diageo

PRICE RANGE
$$

DRINKING RECOMMENDATION

First released in 2016, Bulleit Barrel Strength Bourbon is the latest expression released in the Bulleit line-up. It is likely that the whiskey in the current releases was distilled under contract by Four Roses and matured at the Stitzel-Weller Distillery, owned by Diageo. At some point, Diageo will run out of Four Roses distilled bourbon and will substitute it with whiskey distilled at another undisclosed Kentucky distillery, or, if it can stretch its current stock until 2021, it can start using bourbon made at the Bulleit Distillery in Shelbyville, Kentucky (*see* page 65).

Bulleit Bourbon Barrel Strength Kentucky Straight Bourbon Whiskey

STRENGTH
59.6% ABV (119.2 proof)

MASH BILL
68% corn, 28% rye, 4% malted barley

STILL TYPE
Column still

AGE STATEMENT
NAS

DISTILLERIES
Four Roses Distillery, Lawrenceburg, Kentucky; other undisclosed Kentucky distillery

BRAND OWNER
Diageo

PRICE RANGE
$$$

FLAVOUR The nose on this bourbon is very faint and dense, with only hints of caramel and fruit. With a little time, notes of raisins, plum and honey come through. However, on the palate there is lots of sweetness up front, followed mid-palate by a blanket of charred oak. On the back palate it gets very dry from the oak tannins, although without any bitterness. The finish is a little hot, short and light but without any harshness. Lastly, there is a hint of smokiness from the barrel. Neat, the bourbon is a bit one dimensional, but with a little water the flavour opens up and shows more complexity.

DRINKING RECOMMENDATION

Born in 1830, Edmund Haynes Taylor, Jr became a wealthy Lexington banker and colonel. In 1870, Taylor purchased the Lee's Town Distillery, upgraded the facilities and renamed it the Old Fire Copper Distillery (O.F.C.). In 1878, he sold the distillery to George T. Stagg (*see* page 94) and then, in 1887, he built the Old Taylor Distillery outside Frankfort, Kentucky. Taylor was a strong lobbyist for the industry and used his relationship with US Secretary of the Treasury John Carlisle to craft the 1897 Bottled-in-Bond Act. He also argued for a strict legal definition of bourbon whiskey before President Taft (*see also* pages 17–18). By 1987, Old Taylor Bourbon was in the hands of Jim Beam, who sold it to Sazerac in 2009. The E.H. Taylor bourbons produced by Sazerac are all released as bottled-in-bond.

Colonel E.H. Taylor Small Batch Bottled-in-Bond Kentucky Bourbon

FLAVOUR This bourbon has a light aroma of vanilla and rose petals, followed by a touch of milk chocolate and a hint of orange zest. It tastes slightly sweet and has a smooth texture. While the heat from the 100 proof is noticeable on the first sip, it mellows nicely as you continue to drink. The finish is full of warm spice notes such as cloves and ground ginger, followed by a woody character resembling young pine, with medium tannins that leave the palate dry and waiting for the next sip. This bottling of Colonel Taylor is a solid bourbon and it will hold up well in any bourbon cocktail.

STRENGTH
50% ABV (100 proof)

MASH BILL
Buffalo Trace mash bill #1 (10% or less rye)

STILL TYPE
Column still

AGE STATEMENT
NAS

DISTILLERY
Buffalo Trace Distillery, Frankfort, Kentucky

BRAND OWNER
Sazerac

PRICE RANGE
$$

DRINKING RECOMMENDATION

Established in 2012 by Walter and Kim Catton, Coppercraft Distillery is located in Holland, Michigan, about 48km (30 miles) west of Grand Rapids. Equipped with a 1,325 litre (350 gallon) copper pot still, Coppercraft produces a number of spirits including whiskey, brandy, gin and rum, and is committed to using as many locally grown grains, fruits and herbs as possible. Its bourbon is made from West Michigan corn and rye and is aged for two years before being brought down to 80 proof for bottling. Coppercraft also produces a cask-strength bourbon (*see* page 69) and will be releasing three new bourbons in early 2018.

Coppercraft Straight Bourbon Whiskey

STRENGTH
40% ABV (80 proof)

MASH BILL
70% corn, 25% rye, 5% malted barley

STILL TYPE
Pot still

AGE STATEMENT
2 years

DISTILLERY
Coppercraft Distillery, Holland, Michigan

BRAND OWNER
Coppercraft Distillery

PRICE RANGE
$$

FLAVOUR The nose on this bourbon is light and has a grain-forward character with notes of oak and fresh plum. The palate is smooth and full-bodied, and flavours of oak and grain dominate with an underlying note of fruitiness. The finish is medium-long and has a touch of smoke and oak. The bourbon is pleasantly warm, although without harshness. This is a nice grain-forward bourbon that has good balance and can be sipped neat or used in a cocktail.

DRINKING RECOMMENDATION

Coppercraft Cask Strength Bourbon is distilled from locally grown corn and rye and aged for two years in charred new oak barrels. The bourbon is then dumped and bottled without adding water or chill filtering.

Coppercraft Cask Strength Straight Bourbon Whiskey

FLAVOUR The nose is light and fruity, reminiscent of apples with a touch of oak. With a little bit of water, light floral aromas and notes of vanilla and maple syrup open up. The palate starts sweet with notes of light caramel and then develops a rye spice character followed by oak. Again, with water the sweetness of the bourbon and its fruity character ramps up and the spice disappears. Neat, the finish is very hot, but once that dissipates there are notes of caramel, dark chocolate and baked pear. At cask strength, the bourbon is very hot; however, it shows a nice mix of light fruity flavours and rye spice. Drink it on the rocks or use it in a cocktail that needs a light, fruity bourbon at higher proof.

STRENGTH
58.55% ABV (117.1 proof)

MASH BILL
70% corn, 25% rye, 5% malted barley

STILL TYPE
Pot still

AGE STATEMENT
2 years

DISTILLERY
Coppercraft Distillery, Holland, Michigan

BRAND OWNER
Coppercraft Distillery

PRICE RANGE
$$$

DRINKING RECOMMENDATION

Named for a St. Louis grocer, David Nicholson began sourcing and selling bourbon in 1843. After Prohibition, David Nicholson 1843 Bourbon was made at the famed Stitzel-Weller Distillery in Shively, Kentucky, using its wheated bourbon recipe. In 1972, the distillery was sold and through a series of mergers Diageo became the owner of Stitzel-Weller, which was used to mature whiskey. However, the David Nicholson brand remained with the Van Winkle family. In 2000, it was purchased by Luxco, a spirits company based in St. Louis, Missouri, bringing the brand full circle back to its origins. While Luxco used to disclose that its whiskey came from Heaven Hill Distillery, it no longer discloses the source of its bourbon, although David Nicholson 1843 Bourbon is still being made with a wheated mash.

David Nicholson 1843 Kentucky Straight Bourbon Whiskey

STRENGTH
50% ABV (100 proof)

MASH BILL
Wheated mash

STILL TYPE
Column still

AGE STATEMENT
NAS

DISTILLERY
Undisclosed Kentucky distillery

BRAND OWNER
Luxco

PRICE RANGE
$$

FLAVOUR The bourbon has sweet oatmeal cookies and a little raisin on the nose, before it becomes dry and more woody, with a fruity hint of coconut water and milk. This is a rich, creamy nose with a touch of amaretti. There are bright notes on the palate of stalky, fresh wood, even going toward more vegetal, leafy notes. It grows earthier toward the finish, with notes of dried currants. The finish is full of balanced notes of rye and grain: dark fruit, lasting and earthy dark chocolate, even a hint of chilli. This bourbon would work well in short, rich cocktails like a Manhattan or Boulevardier.

DRINKING RECOMMENDATION

First released in 2016, David Nicholson Reserve Bourbon is made using an extra-aged "ryed" bourbon. Like the 1843 (*see* page 70), Luxco sources this bourbon from an undisclosed Kentucky distillery, vatting it and bottling at 100 proof.

David Nicholson Reserve Kentucky Straight Bourbon Whiskey

FLAVOUR A sweet and inviting nose of brown sugar cookies with raisins and currants, it takes on a slight rum-like character with light notes of banana and caramel shards. The palate is warming, but clean with notes of grain, currants and lightly caramelized banana, and a warm spice toward the finish. The finish is full of dry grain and wood notes, which are perfectly balanced between the fresh notes of light oak and the heavier, more caramelized wood flavours. This is a balanced bourbon with a distinctive rum-like character to start, followed by an array of solid, well-integrated wood notes on the finish.

STRENGTH
50% ABV (100 proof)

MASH BILL
Rye mash

STILL TYPE
Column still

AGE STATEMENT
NAS

DISTILLERY
Undisclosed Kentucky distillery

BRAND OWNER
Luxco

PRICE RANGE
$$

DRINKING RECOMMENDATION

Do Good Distillery was founded in 2013 by Jim and Liz Harrelson. The distillery name comes from a Benjamin Franklin quote that serves as the company's motto, "You do well, by doing good". Jim had served for 14 years as a sheriff's deputy until he was inspired in part by the death of his brother-in-law to act on his dream of operating a craft distillery. Harrelson jumped into the deep end, making seven whiskeys, two rums and a gin. One of these whiskeys was Nighthawk Bourbon, which at present is a two-year-old pot-distilled whiskey from a rye mash. The bourbon uses the nickname for Jim's brother-in-law and is made with 100% California-grown grains, including merced rye grown in Modesto.

Do Good Nighthawk Bourbon Whisky

STRENGTH
45.55% ABV (91.1 proof)

MASH BILL
Rye mash

STILL TYPE
Pot still

AGE STATEMENT
2 years

DISTILLERY
Do Good Distillery, Modesto, California

BRAND OWNER
Do Good Distillery

PRICE RANGE
$$

FLAVOUR This bourbon has a powerful and fragrant aroma that pours out of the glass with notes of vanilla, sweet cherries, oak, cedar, dry hay and corn husks. The flavour is slightly grassy with a spiciness from the young oak and grain followed by roasted corn. In the mouth the bourbon has a nice medium-to-full body and rounds out with a light sweetness of plums and stone fruit. The finish is warm and dry with light oakiness and the flavour of brown sugar, although without any sweetness. Although this is a young whiskey, it has lots of promise and should work well on the rocks, in a Highball or where a more grain-forward bourbon is needed for your cocktail.

DRINKING RECOMMENDATION

Do Good California Bourbon is a two-year-old whiskey, pot-distilled from a wheated mash. Like Do Good's Nighthawk Bourbon (*see* page 72), all of the grains used are grown in California. After the barrels reach maturity, they are dumped and the bourbon is reduced in strength to 91.1 proof. This is a subtle nod to the emergency services and the fact that founder Jim Harrelson was once a sheriff's deputy.

Do Good California Bourbon Whisky

FLAVOUR The nose has a sweetness to it with aromas of vanilla, caramel and cinnamon, and a light fruitiness reminiscent of brandied cherries. Once it has time to breathe, oak and notes like dry cornmeal come to the forefront. The palate is soft and buttery with dry oak tannins, followed by caramel and dark dried cherries that are lightly sweet. The finish is slightly warm and medium-dry, with some oaky bitterness followed by lingering flavours of sweet vanilla and a hint of baking spices. While this bourbon still tastes young at two years old, it shows promise for the future and will work well in cocktails with vermouth.

STRENGTH
45.55% ABV (91.1 proof)

MASH BILL
Wheated mash

STILL TYPE
Pot still

AGE STATEMENT
2 years

DISTILLERY
Do Good Distillery, Modesto, California

BRAND OWNER
Do Good Distillery

PRICE RANGE
$$

DRINKING RECOMMENDATION

Dry Fly Bourbon 101 was the first legal bourbon made in the state of Washington. The Dry Fly distillery was founded by two friends, Don Poffenroth and Kent Fleischmann, who developed the idea for opening a craft distillery while fly fishing. From their love of the outdoors, Don and Kent have committed to use locally sourced grains grown by farmers in Eastern Washington. Their wheated bourbon is pot distilled and matured for at least three years before the whiskey is vatted and reduced in strength to 101 proof. In 2011, Dry Fly Distilling was named Distillery of the Year by the American Distilling Institute.

Dry Fly Bourbon 101 Straight Bourbon Whiskey

STRENGTH
50.5% ABV (101 proof)

MASH BILL
60% corn, 20% wheat, 20% malted barley

STILL TYPE
Pot still

AGE STATEMENT
4 years

DISTILLERY
Dry Fly Distilling, Spokane, Washington

BRAND OWNER
Dry Fly Distilling

PRICE RANGE
$$

FLAVOUR The nose has an aroma of brown sugar, with light floral aromatics followed by green oak and roasted corn in the husk. The palate is full-bodied and simultaneously sweet and spicy, with notes of nutmeg and cloves followed by dried cherries, caramel and a touch of spice from the grain. The finish has some heat followed by a nice balance of sweetness and oak. As the finish lingers, notes of baked apple and apple butter (thick, caramelized apple sauce) mingle with tobacco. This is an enjoyable bourbon to drink neat if you tend toward high-proof or cask-strength bourbons. Otherwise, a little water or ice will work well. It would also show well in a number of classic cocktails with absinthe.

DRINKING RECOMMENDATION

First released in the 1970s, Eagle Rare Bourbon was introduced right on the cusp of the great whiskey decline. Originally owned by Seagram, it sold the brand in 1989 to Sazerac, who at the time did not own its own distillery, but sourced whiskey from Heaven Hill Distillery. In 1992, Sazerac bought the George T. Stagg Distillery (*see* page 94) and spent considerable time renovating it. Today, Eagle Rare comes in two expressions: a 10-year-old and a 17-year-old bourbon, both bottled at 90 proof.

Eagle Rare Kentucky Straight Bourbon Whiskey

FLAVOUR The nose is light, with notes of vanilla and fresh plum skins and an underlying oak character. The palate is sweet with flavours of soft red apple and fresh cherries, followed by dry oak. The finish is medium-long and smooth with no heat or burn. As the whiskey dissipates, flavours of mature oak and baking spices are followed by a lingering sweetness. This is a truly great bourbon that is well balanced and a touch on the sweet side. It is great neat or with a drop of water, and it is excellent in high-end cocktails.

STRENGTH
45% ABV (90 proof)

MASH BILL
Buffalo Trace mash bill #1 (10% or less rye)

STILL TYPE
Column still

AGE STATEMENT
10 years

DISTILLERY
Buffalo Trace Distillery, Frankfort, Kentucky

BRAND OWNER
Sazerac

PRICE RANGE
$$

DRINKING RECOMMENDATION

Elijah Craig was a Virginian and a Baptist preacher who moved to Kentucky sometime around the end of the 18th century. Bourbon legend claims he was the first distiller to use charred oak barrels to store his corn whiskey, hence making bourbon. However, there is no historical evidence to back up these claims, although it is likely that Elijah Craig did make some sort of corn whiskey. In honour of this historic figure, Heaven Hill first released 12-year-old Elijah Craig Small Batch Bourbon in 1986. By 2016, it had become so popular that Heaven Hill decided to remove the whiskey's age statement so that it could be pulled from barrels that were eight years and older.

Elijah Craig Small Batch Kentucky Straight Bourbon Whiskey

STRENGTH
47% ABV (94 proof)

MASH BILL
78% corn, 10% rye, 12% malted barley

STILL TYPE
Column still

AGE STATEMENT
NAS

DISTILLERY
Heaven Hill Distillery, Bardstown, Kentucky

BRAND OWNER
Heaven Hill Distillery

PRICE RANGE
$$

FLAVOUR The bourbon has a strong aroma of caramel and vanilla, with notes of fresh oak and green apples. The palate is intense, full of sweet caramel, oak and baking spices. At 47% ABV, there is some heat but very little astringency and the flavours round out with a pleasant note of honey water. The finish starts with a lingering sweetness that is balanced with dry tannins from the oak. Spice flavours and cornbread slowly fade as a warm sensation fills your chest. This is a very bold bourbon that should please drinkers who like stronger wood and oak notes in their whiskey. Its power is awe-inspiring; it is definitely a bourbon worth contemplating slowly over a long, quiet evening.

DRINKING RECOMMENDATION

Elijah Craig Barrel Proof carries a 12-year-age statement and comes from bottling one barrel of 12-year-old-whiskey without any additions, even water. Each bottle comes with a batch label such as A117. The letter corresponds with the number of the bottling run for the year: A=1st, B=2nd etc. The first number corresponds to the month the bourbon was bottled and the last two numbers correspond with the year. So A117 was the first run of Elijah Craig Barrel Proof bottled in January 2017.

Elijah Craig Barrel Proof Small Batch Kentucky Straight Bourbon Whiskey

FLAVOUR Served neat, the nose is closed with a strong aroma of alcohol and green barrel notes with not much else. With a little added water the bourbon opens to show some caramel, cinnamon and dried fruit notes. On the palate the bourbon is sweet on the entry and quickly dries from all the alcohol. It has pleasant rich flavours of vanilla and caramel; with water, oak and strong secondary notes of tobacco and dried orange coming through. Not surprisingly, the finish is very dry with a little bit of oak and not much else. With water, the finish is still warm although much more manageable. Oak continues to dominate and there are faint notes of fruit that linger on the tongue. Do not drink it neat but rather pour over ice or add water. This will open up a nice oak-forward bourbon with warm spice and fruit notes.

STRENGTH
63.5% ABV (127 proof)

MASH BILL
78% corn, 10% rye, 12% malted barley

STILL TYPE
Column still

AGE STATEMENT
12 years

DISTILLERY
Heaven Hill Distillery, Bardstown, Kentucky

BRAND OWNER
Heaven Hill Distillery

PRICE RANGE
$$$

DRINKING RECOMMENDATION

Elijah Craig Single Barrel Bourbon, aged for 18 years, has become very difficult to find, like many other extra-aged bourbons, and as a result prices have risen. This bourbon is a very good testament to the quality of the whiskey produced at Heaven Hill, as well as its barrel management.

Elijah Craig Single Barrel Kentucky Straight Bourbon Whiskey Aged 18 Years

STRENGTH
45% ABV (90 proof)

MASH BILL
78% corn, 10% rye, 12% malted barley

STILL TYPE
Column still

AGE STATEMENT
18 years

DISTILLERY
Heaven Hill Distillery, Bardstown, Kentucky

BRAND OWNER
Heaven Hill Distillery

PRICE RANGE
$$$$$

FLAVOUR The nose has a light note of bubble gum and dried cherries, with a hint of oak. As the whiskey breathes, notes of vanilla and sweet caramel come to the forefront also with a hint of oak. The finish is dry and long with a dominant oak note and an underlying sweetness of vanilla, a touch of bright fruit and a flash of heat that quickly fades. While the bourbon is oak forward, it is very well balanced for its age and very well structured. Drink it neat.

DRINKING RECOMMENDATION

At 23 years old, each bottle of Elijah Craig Single Barrel 23 comes from one barrel and is in a very elite club. Not many bourbon barrels can age for this long. Many would become over-oaked and virtually undrinkable. However, using its barrel management, Heaven Hill is able to identify those casks that show the potential to go the distance and become some of the finest and most long-aged American whiskey.

Elijah Craig Single Barrel Kentucky Straight Bourbon Whiskey Aged 23 Years

FLAVOUR The nose is incredibly rich and concentrated with notes of dried fruit, rum and raisin, vanilla and caramel, followed by a light, bright note of alcohol. The flavour of the bourbon is excellent, full of sweetness, oak, dried fruit, cherries, plum and mixed spice. The finish is long and dry, dominated by vanilla, rum and raisin and sweet cherries. Elijah Craig 23 is a rich and decadent bourbon that is both very sweet and well balanced with dryness from the oak. As the flavour fades, oak shines through. Definitely drink it neat and savour the rich complexity that comes from 23 years of developing and concentrating flavour in an oak barrel.

STRENGTH
45% ABV (90 proof)

MASH BILL
78% corn, 10% rye, 12% malted barley

STILL TYPE
Column still

AGE STATEMENT
23 years

DISTILLERY
Heaven Hill Distillery, Bardstown, Kentucky

BRAND OWNER
Heaven Hill Distillery

PRICE RANGE
$$$$$

DRINKING RECOMMENDATION

Elmer T. Lee began working at the Albert B. Blanton Distillery (now Buffalo Trace) in 1949 and continued there until he retired as Master Distiller in 1985. Lee was responsible for the creation of the first-ever single barrel bourbon, which he named after Albert Blanton (*see* page 60). For his innovative work and leadership in the bourbon industry, Lee was inducted into the Bourbon Hall of Fame in 2001. To honour his accomplishments, Age International and Sazerac have released a single barrel bourbon in Lee's name, made from a well-aged barrel of the Buffalo Trace mash bill #2 and bottled at 90 proof.

Elmer T. Lee Single Barrel Sour Mash Kentucky Straight Bourbon Whiskey

STRENGTH
45% ABV (90 proof)

MASH BILL
Buffalo Trace mash bill #2
(12–15% rye)

STILL TYPE
Column still

AGE STATEMENT
NAS

DISTILLERY
Buffalo Trace Distillery,
Frankfort, Kentucky

BRAND OWNER
Age International

PRICE RANGE
$$$$

FLAVOUR The nose is bright and sweet, with notes of fresh plum and an underlying character of caramel and vanilla. The palate is very smooth with a note of tropical fruit, followed by milk chocolate and a hint of caramel. The finish is light, short and semidry, with a lingering note of oak. Overall, it is an excellent bourbon, bright and fruity, and should only be drunk neat.

DRINKING RECOMMENDATION

Launched in 1957, Evan Williams Black Label is Heaven Hill's flagship brand. Evan Williams, for whom the bourbon is named, was a distiller born in Wales, who settled in the Virginia frontier. He built a distillery in Louisville on the Ohio River. While Heaven Hill likes to claim that Evan Williams was Kentucky's first distillery, there is little to no historical evidence to support this claim. That being said, Evan Williams Bourbon is an excellent product and, in 2016, Heaven Hill sold over $50 million worth of its whiskey. And, while Evan Williams Black Label used to carry a seven-year age statement, this has been dropped to allow Heaven Hill to pull from slightly younger barrels, while maintaining its quality and price point.

Evan Williams Black Label Kentucky Straight Bourbon Whiskey

FLAVOUR The nose has strong notes of oak, cherries and vanilla. As the bourbon breathes, aromas of green apple and minerally Chardonnay come forward. On the palate the whiskey is smooth, with a medium body and a pleasant warmth that fills the mouth. The bourbon tastes lightly sweet with notes of oak, fresh bread and mixed spice. On the finish the bready character lingers, while higher notes of sweet cherry shine through and a light oak astringency dries the mouth. This is a high-quality everyday bourbon that's easy on the bank account and is great for those who are not enamoured with the extra-aged, oak-forward bourbons that seem to be all the rage. This bourbon works neat and is excellent mixed in cocktails.

STRENGTH
43% ABV (86 proof)

MASH BILL
78% corn, 10% rye, 12% malted barley

STILL TYPE
Column still

AGE STATEMENT
NAS

DISTILLERY
Heaven Hill Distillery, Bardstown, Kentucky

BRAND OWNER
Heaven Hill Distillery

PRICE RANGE
$

DRINKING RECOMMENDATION

Evan Williams White Label is a bottled-in-bond expression of the line; therefore, we know that the whiskey is at least four years old, distilled at Heaven Hill, all in the same season and bottled at 100 proof. While the White Label is not quite as common as the Black Label (*see* page 81), it is a bold bourbon with a good strength for making spirit-forward cocktails.

Evan Williams White Label Bottled-in-Bond Kentucky Straight Bourbon Whiskey

STRENGTH
50% ABV (100 proof)

MASH BILL
78% corn, 10% rye, 12% malted barley

STILL TYPE
Column still

AGE STATEMENT
NAS

DISTILLERY
Heaven Hill Distillery, Bardstown, Kentucky

BRAND OWNER
Heaven Hill Distillery

PRICE RANGE
$

FLAVOUR While the nose is a little closed, there are bright and fruity aromas of apple, cinnamon and just a touch of oak. On the palate the bourbon is smooth and grassy with a semisweet flavour of apples and peaches. The finish has some heat and is long and dry from the oak tannins. As the whiskey lingers there are notes of apple skins and wet grass drying on a warm morning. Because of the heat, most will not want to drink this neat but opt for using it in a tall cocktail that calls for a bourbon that is drier.

DRINKING RECOMMENDATION

Evan Williams 1783 Small Batch Bourbon is said to be made in batches of no more than 80 barrels at one time. The date is meant to commemorate the year that Evan Williams became Kentucky's first distiller (*see* page 81). While it is possible that Evan Williams began distilling in 1783, there is no historical evidence that he was the first distiller in the state.

Evan Williams 1783 Small Batch Sour Mash Kentucky Straight Bourbon Whiskey

FLAVOUR This bourbon has a light nose with notes of caramel and vanilla, followed by mixed spice and oak, then the aroma is rounded out with a pleasant note of fresh green apple. The palate is smooth with a full body and slightly sweet. The bourbon has flavours of vanilla with a hint of spice and baked apple supported by a strong oak character. The finish is long, soft and dry. While oak flavours dominate the finish there are also hints of vanilla and red cherries. This is a much more oak-forward expression of Evan Williams and is recommended for those who want a little bit more wood flavour than in the regular Black Label. The bourbon works well neat or in a cocktail that needs a drier, wood-forward bourbon.

STRENGTH
43% ABV (86 proof)

MASH BILL
78% corn, 10% rye, 12% malted barley

STILL TYPE
Column still

AGE STATEMENT
NAS

DISTILLERY
Heaven Hill Distillery, Bardstown, Kentucky

BRAND OWNER
Heaven Hill Distillery

PRICE RANGE
$

DRINKING RECOMMENDATION

Heaven Hill released its first single barrel vintage bourbon in 1995. While this was not the first single barrel bourbon ever released, the distillery distinguished its product by only selecting barrels from the same year the bourbon was put in oak. Many other single barrel whiskeys are selected from barrels based on a similar flavour profile rather than age. Each year, Heaven Hill's Master Distiller selects "honey" barrels that come from the upper floors of its rickhouses. He explains that these upper floors experience the greatest annual temperature swings, which the distillery believes results in a bourbon that is deeper in colour and richer in flavour. While earlier vintages came in at nine or ten years old, the most recent expression was put in oak in 2009, making it seven to eight years old at the most.

Evan Williams Single Barrel Vintage Kentucky Straight Bourbon Whiskey

STRENGTH
43.3% ABV (86.6 proof)

MASH BILL
78% corn, 10% rye, 12% malted barley

STILL TYPE
Column still

AGE STATEMENT
NAS

DISTILLERY
Heaven Hill Distillery, Bardstown, Kentucky

BRAND OWNER
Heaven Hill Distillery

PRICE RANGE
$$

FLAVOUR The nose is rich and powerful, full of caramel and vanilla with undertones of cedar, sweet cherries and persimmons. The palate is surprisingly light and delicate, although the alcohol is initially a little strong. The bourbon is slightly sweet and fruity; however, it is well balanced with oak. The finish has a light dryness from the oak that initially tastes slightly nutty and salty. As the flavours linger, sweet notes of raspberries and cherries come back to the fore. With its lighter and more delicate flavours, this is a great bourbon to sip neat, especially for its sub $30 price tag. Given a little time to breathe in the glass, some of the strong alcohol notes that are initially intense blow off and you are left with a pleasant and smooth bourbon. That being said, barrel bottled is likely to vary slightly across bottlings.

DRINKING RECOMMENDATION

Founded in 2011 by Paul Hletko in Evanston, Illinois, FEW Spirits has blazed a bold path in the craft distilling world. In a subtle jab at the failure of National Prohibition, FEW Spirits is named after Frances Elizabeth Willard, one of the founding members of the Women's Christian Temperance Union. FEW makes all of its spirits from grain to glass and sources much of its grain from regional farmers; its barrels come from a cooperage in Minnesota. The bourbon is first distilled on a column still and then distilled a second time on a pot still. It is then barrelled and matured for at least one year.

FEW Bourbon Whiskey

FLAVOUR The bourbon has a soft and muted nose, but one full of genuine notes of oak, which is reminiscent of walking into a rackhouse. This is accompanied by notes of black tea with lemon, light brown sugar and maple syrup, and a light, woody nuttiness that reminds me of acorns or hazelnuts. On the palate, it is smooth, but textured, robust and pleasantly dry – almost bitter at the start – but as it warms, creamier oak and vanilla flavours unfold, accompanied by notes of freshly baked bread. The finish is dry and woody, but full-bodied, like an espresso with whiskey and cream. This is a good, solid bourbon that would be great for someone who enjoys the category but wants to explore the next level of the spirit.

STRENGTH
46.5% ABV (93 proof)

MASH BILL
70% corn, 20% rye, 10% malted barley

STILL TYPE
Column and pot stills

AGE STATEMENT
1 year

DISTILLERY
FEW Spirits, Evanston, Illinois

BRAND OWNER
FEW Spirits

PRICE RANGE
$$

DRINKING RECOMMENDATION

Founded in 2012, That Boutique-y Whisky Company is an independent bottler of fine whiskeys from around the world. While most of its selections focus on Scotch whisky, it has released a couple of bourbons, including one from FEW Spirits. This expression of FEW Bourbon is aged for two years and bottled at 103.6 proof.

FEW Bourbon from That Boutique-y Whisky Company

STRENGTH
51.8% ABV (103.6 proof)

MASH BILL
Wheated mash

STILL TYPE
Column and pot stills

AGE STATEMENT
2 years

DISTILLERY
FEW Spirits, Evanston, Illinois

BRAND OWNER
That Boutique-y Whisky Company

PRICE RANGE
$$$

FLAVOUR The bourbon is hugely complex on the nose, with notes of marzipan, yeast-heavy sweet bread and toffee, accompanied by tart notes of blackberry, apple, almond and a hint of coffee. Occasionally, the notes combine to produce aromas of sweet tobacco. To taste, this is powerful and peppery from the start, before growing dry, spicy and increasingly creamy, with flavours of light banana bread and honey rings breakfast cereal. The finish is clean and particularly dry, with notes of vanilla and oak and hints of milk chocolate and cherry wood. A flavourful and colourful bourbon full of genuine wood notes, best savoured neat.

DRINKING RECOMMENDATION

Originally founded by Rufus Mathewson Rose in Atlanta, Georgia, the Four Roses Distillery and its whiskey was trademarked by Paul Jones, Jr in 1888. In 1922, the Paul Jones Company bought the Frankfort Distilling Company, giving it control of its own supply, which it sold during Prohibition for "medicinal purposes". By 1943 the Four Roses Distillery had been sold to Seagram, which pulled it from the USA in the late 1950s to focus in Europe and Asia. In 2002, Four Roses was purchased by the Kirin Brewery Company, and two years later Four Roses Bourbon was once again sold in the US. Four Roses makes bourbon using two mash bills and five yeast strains, each of which is distilled and barrelled individually. For Four Roses Yellow Label, all ten of these bourbons are blended together and bottled at 80 proof.

Four Roses Yellow Label Kentucky Straight Bourbon Whiskey

FLAVOUR The nose opens with notes of vanilla, oak and rye spice. As the whiskey breathes, a hint of sweet cherries and caramel round out the aroma. On the palate there is some heat, followed by light flavours of caramel and oak, with just a hint of cocoa powder. The finish is semidry with light oak flavours and a touch of astringency. Overall, Four Roses Yellow Label is a classic value bourbon that can be drunk neat but is best in cocktails like a Manhattan or an Old Fashioned.

STRENGTH
40% ABV (80 proof)

MASH BILL
67.5% corn, 27.5% rye, 5% malted barley

STILL TYPE
Column still

AGE STATEMENT
NAS

DISTILLERY
Four Roses Distillery, Lawrenceburg, Kentucky

BRAND OWNER
Kirin Brewery Company

PRICE RANGE
$

DRINKING RECOMMENDATION

First released in September 2006, Four Roses Small Batch Bourbon is a blend of four bourbons produced at the distillery using both mash bills E and B and two yeast strains, K and O. According to the distillery, yeast strain K is meant to add light spice caramel flavours, while yeast strain O is meant to emphasize rich fruitiness as well as light caramel and vanilla notes. The bourbons are aged for less than seven years, vatted and bottled at 90 proof.

Four Roses Small Batch Kentucky Straight Bourbon Whiskey

STRENGTH
45% ABV (90 proof)

MASH BILL
67.5% corn, 27.5% rye, 5% malted barley

STILL TYPE
Column still

AGE STATEMENT
NAS

DISTILLERY
Four Roses Distillery, Lawrenceburg, Kentucky

BRAND OWNER
Kirin Brewery Company

PRICE RANGE
$$

FLAVOUR Immediately on the nose there are fruity notes and a whiff of acetone. Underneath these initial aromas are notes of burnt oak and a strong presence of vanilla. On the palate the first taste is a slightly astringent green note that is then followed by light heat on the tongue. After the heat dissipates, you notice both a sweetness and a big wallop of spice. After swallowing, the bourbon lingers for a long time with clear notes of oak and vanilla. This small batch bourbon has some nice qualities: it is well balanced and it is an easy-to-drink bourbon well worth its price tag.

DRINKING RECOMMENDATION

Founded in 2004 by Dan Garrison in Hye, Texas, Garrison Brothers Distillery distilled its first new-make whiskey in 2008 and, after two years in the barrel, bottled the first batch of its Texas Straight Bourbon in 2010. Garrison took his time learning his craft and developed a wheated bourbon that could withstand ageing in the intense cold and heat of the Texas Hill Country and still remain balanced. Unlike many other craft distillers who make whiskey, gin and vodka, Garrison Brothers only makes bourbon and its dedication to that purpose shows in the whiskey. The current release of the straight bourbon was matured for three years, vatted and brought down to 94 proof using rainwater.

Garrison Brothers Texas Straight Bourbon Whiskey

FLAVOUR This bourbon has a rich nose of caramel with underlying notes of cinnamon, cardamom and oak. The palate is sweet and smooth with really nice spice notes of cinnamon and just a touch of oak. The finish is long, warm and semisweet, with notes of caramel balanced with oak tannins. Overall, this is a very likeable bourbon full of baking spices and caramel and just a touch of young oak. This would probably be enjoyed by those who like sweet and spice-forward bourbon. Drink it neat or in a cocktail where you want to amplify the spice character of the aromatic bitters.

STRENGTH
47% ABV (94 proof)

MASH BILL
74% #1 Panhandle white corn, 15% red winter wheat, 11% malted barley

STILL TYPE
Pot still

AGE STATEMENT
3 years

DISTILLERY
Garrison Brothers Distillery, Hye, Texas

BRAND OWNER
Garrison Brothers Distillery

PRICE RANGE
$$$$

DRINKING RECOMMENDATION

The Garrison Brothers Single Barrel Texas Straight Bourbon is a fantastic example of the excellent production methods used to make the whiskey. There is no way to hide any potential flaws because all of the spirit comes from one barrel and is reduced in strength with rainwater.

Garrison Brothers Single Barrel Texas Straight Bourbon Whiskey

STRENGTH
47% ABV (94 proof)

MASH BILL
74% #1 Panhandle white corn, 15% red winter wheat, 11% malted barley

STILL TYPE
Pot still

AGE STATEMENT
3 years

DISTILLERY
Garrison Brothers Distillery, Hye, Texas

BRAND OWNER
Garrison Brothers Distillery

PRICE RANGE
$$$$

FLAVOUR The Single Barrel has a very rich nose with dark aromas of vanilla, dried fruit and tobacco balanced with nice wood notes of cedar and oak. The palate is very pleasant, with notes of smoke, salted caramel and oak, and the finish is long, warm and dry, with notes of seasoned oak, caramel and dark chocolate. This is an excellent bourbon especially at only three years old. It is rich in flavour, incredibly smooth at 94 proof and well worth the investment if you are looking to splurge a little. Drink neat and enjoy.

DRINKING RECOMMENDATION

A German-born immigrant, George Dickel settled in Nashville, Tennessee, and sold whiskey sourced from local distillers. In 1888, George A. Dickel & Company became the sole distributor for Cascade Whisky made outside Tullahoma, Tennessee. However, in 1910, Tennessee enacted statewide Prohibition of alcohol so the then owner Victor Emmanuel Shwab moved production to the Stitzel Distillery in Louisville, Kentucky. After Prohibition, Shwab sold Cascade Whisky to the Schenley Distilling Company who made a product called Geo and began production in a new distillery in 1959. George Dickel Tennessee Whisky was first bottled in 1964 and through a series of mergers and acquisitions Diageo became the owner of the Cascade Hollow Distillery and George Dickel in 1997.

George Dickel Sour Mash Tennessee Whisky Superior No. 12

FLAVOUR The whiskey has a muted nose with light notes of unfiltered (cloudy) apple juice and just a touch of alcohol. This light-bodied whiskey is sweet on the palate with a little bit of oak and a hit of fruitiness. The finish is short and has notes of apple and oak and then it's done. George Dickel No. 12 is a simple and easy-to-drink whiskey. While it does not have a ton of character compared to some Kentucky bourbons, it still works neat, on the rocks or in your favourite tall drink or even a Manhattan. For the price, I think it is a nice, inexpensive whiskey.

STRENGTH
45% ABV (90 proof)

MASH BILL
84% corn, 8% rye, 8% malted barley

STILL TYPE
Column still

AGE STATEMENT
NAS

DISTILLERY
George A. Dickel & Co., Tullahoma, Tennessee

BRAND OWNER
Diageo

PRICE RANGE
$$

DRINKING RECOMMENDATION

Like all George Dickel whiskeys, the Classic No. 8 Tennessee Whisky is distilled from a rye mash in a 107cm (42 inch) diameter column still to 135 proof. After coming off the still, the new-make whiskey is cooled to 4.4°C (40°F) and treated with the Lincoln County Process (*see* page 41). Diageo adds the unaged spirit to vats of sugar maple charcoal and lets it sit for about a week before draining and barrelling it. Once the barrels are mature, they are dumped and reduced in strength to 80 proof for the No. 8 brand. Dickel produces five other Tennessee whiskeys, including Superior No. 12 (90 proof – *see* page 91).

George Dickel Sour Mash Tennessee Whisky Classic No. 8

STRENGTH
40% ABV (80 proof)

MASH BILL
84% corn, 8% rye, 8% malted barley

STILL TYPE
Column still

AGE STATEMENT
NAS

DISTILLERY
George A. Dickel & Co., Tullahoma, Tennessee

BRAND OWNER
Diageo

PRICE RANGE
$

FLAVOUR The nose has nice notes of unfiltered (cloudy) apple juice and pear, with a light aroma of caramel and oak lingering in the background. In the mouth, George Dickel No. 8 has a pleasant light body with light flavours of caramel, cinnamon, fruit and oak. The finish is soft, sweet and long, with lingering notes of caramel, cinnamon, oak and pear. This is a very enjoyable, light-flavoured whiskey that is slightly sweet and fruity. Excellent neat, it would also be great in tall, refreshing cocktails.

DRINKING RECOMMENDATION

The George Dickel Barrel Select Tennessee Whisky has no age statement, although its owner Diageo claims that each batch of the whiskey comes only from ten barrels aged between ten and twelve years. Once the barrels are vatted, the whiskey is reduced in strength to 86 proof before bottling.

George Dickel Barrel Select Tennessee Whisky

FLAVOUR This bourbon has nice aromas of sweet cherries, vanilla and oak, with a touch of wood smoke in the background. On the entry, the whiskey is sweet and well balanced with notes of spice, caramel sweetness and oak. Overall, the flavours are very well integrated. The finish is semisweet with notes of vanilla and fruit, followed by pleasant notes of tobacco and spice and a gentle warmth from the alcohol, although it is not harsh in any way. The Barrel Select is an excellent Tennessee whiskey that is a pleasure to drink neat. Overall, it is very well balanced and it is likely that both sweet bourbon drinkers and oak bourbon drinkers would like it. You could drink this on the rocks if you like, though it doesn't need dilution. As for cocktails, it would make a great Manhattan or any other drink that calls for vermouth.

STRENGTH
43% ABV (86 proof)

MASH BILL
84% corn, 8% rye, 8% malted barley

STILL TYPE
Column still

AGE STATEMENT
NAS

DISTILLERY
George A. Dickel & Co., Tullahoma, Tennessee

BRAND OWNER
Diageo

PRICE RANGE
$$

DRINKING RECOMMENDATION

George T. Stagg was born in Garrard County, Kentucky, in 1835. In 1878 he purchased the O.F.C. Distillery from Colonel E. H. Taylor, Jr, but by 1886, Stagg and Taylor had fallen out and Taylor left to start a new distillery of his own (*see* page 67). Meanwhile, Stagg continued to grow the business and in 1904 he renamed the distillery after himself. In 1992, Sazerac purchased the Stagg distillery and around 1999 introduced its Antique Collection, which includes five whiskeys, one of which is George T. Stagg Bourbon (*see also* Eagle Rare, page 75). It is made using the #1 mash bill and bottled at barrel proof, which varies from year to year.

George T. Stagg Kentucky Straight Bourbon Whiskey

STRENGTH
69.1% ABV (138.2 proof)

MASH BILL
Buffalo Trace mash bill #1
(10% or less rye)

STILL TYPE
Column still

AGE STATEMENT
NAS

DISTILLERY
Buffalo Trace Distillery,
Frankfort, Kentucky

BRAND OWNER
Sazerac

PRICE RANGE
$$$$$

FLAVOUR This bourbon has a rich nose of caramel and vanilla with an underlying aroma of oak, followed by a note of alcohol, although this is not as strong as you would expect. It takes a couple of sips for your tongue to acclimatize to the alcohol's strength. Once there, notes of caramel and vanilla come through, although these are very light in character. The finish is short and initially very dry and clean because of the high proof. A sense of sweetness and a hint of vanilla and sweet cherries linger. With water the flavours open up and the bourbon still retains its light character. I would suggest drinking this with water – neat it is very intense and a little lacking in depth. If you prefer simple, well-balanced flavours in your bourbon and don't mind adding a little water, search it out.

DRINKING RECOMMENDATION

Gun Fighter American Bourbon is sourced and finished by Maison De La Vie Ltd at its Golden Moon Distillery in Golden, Colorado. The distillery was founded by Stephen Gould and Karen Knight in 2008 and specializes in making spirits based on historical recipes that utilize processes and methods used by distillers over the past 200 years. They own four antique stills as well as an impressive collection of rare books on distilling. As for the bourbon, the young whiskey is sourced from another distillery and matured in charred new American oak barrels for six months at the Golden Moon Distillery. The whiskey is then finished in barrels that previously held French port, adding a unique richness and complexity that also reflect the distillery's historical focus.

Gun Fighter American Bourbon Whiskey Double Cask

FLAVOUR This bourbon has an indulgent nose of sweet caramel, strawberry and raspberry that develops into notes of salted caramel, oak, sticky toffee pudding, a little raisin and breadiness. The complexity continues on the palate, which has a thick texture and flavours of bready grain, followed by caramelized pecans, fudge and pancakes with maple syrup. It grows gradually drier on the palate, with notes of oak, vanilla and butterscotch, all before a lasting and refreshingly dry but fruity finish of spice and red grapes. A rich and full-bodied bourbon with great complexity and balanced sweetness, explore it on its own or with a dash of water, or enjoy it in cocktails like an Old Fashioned.

STRENGTH
50% ABV (100 proof)

MASH BILL
60% corn, 34% rye, 6% malted barley

STILL TYPE
Column still

AGE STATEMENT
6 months

DISTILLERY
Undisclosed distillery

BRAND OWNER
Golden Moon Distillery

PRICE RANGE
$$

DRINKING RECOMMENDATION

In 1939, Heaven Hill Distillery released Old Heaven Hill, its first bottled-in-bond bourbon. Since then the brand has persisted even though it was supplanted in 1957 when Heaven Hill decided to make Evan Williams its flagship brand (*see* page 81). Heaven Hill Bottled-in-Bond Bourbon is typically only available in Kentucky and a few other US states so it may not be easy to find.

Heaven Hill Bottled-in-Bond Old Style Bourbon 6 Years Old

STRENGTH
50% ABV (100 proof)

MASH BILL
78% corn, 10% rye, 12% malted barley

STILL TYPE
Column still

AGE STATEMENT
6 years

DISTILLERY
Heaven Hill Distillery, Bardstown, Kentucky

BRAND OWNER
Heaven Hill Distillery

PRICE RANGE
$

FLAVOUR After the pour the nose is surprisingly closed off despite the high ABV. Once it has had time to breathe, it opens up with aromas of oak, apple, brown sugar, pumpkin bread and maraschino. On the palate this is a little astringent from the oak tannins. It starts warm and crescendos to a nice, not overpowering, level. In the mouth, flavours of cocoa, cinnamon and nutmeg play against a pleasant sweetness and are balanced with the oak. The bourbon has a long finish and while the warmth from the alcohol lingers, notes of sweet maraschino fade into dry oak. With a little bit of water more notes of caramel, toffee and hazelnut come through and interestingly, the oak flavour intensifies. Taken neat the bourbon is a little too hot and slightly bitter. However, it is a solid-value bourbon and works well in classic whiskey cocktails.

DRINKING RECOMMENDATION

In 1837, Henry McKenna was an Irish distiller who completed his journey to America and settled near Fairfield, Kentucky. In honour of his memory, Heaven Hill produces two expressions of Henry McKenna: the first is a standard NAS 80 proof straight bourbon and the second is this ten-year-old single barrel straight bourbon bottled at 100 proof, which is a classic bourbon and incredibly well priced for its age.

Henry McKenna Single Barrel Bottled-in-Bond Kentucky Straight Bourbon Whiskey

FLAVOUR The nose is inviting with aromas of cocoa, baked apple, cinnamon and vanilla and a nice backbone of oak. The palate is sweet, smooth and dry, with rich flavours of sweet almond, caramel and plum jam. These flavour combinations remind me of a classic Mai Tai cocktail only drier. The finish is long and dry, with lingering notes of sweetness and oak and a light heat. Drink it neat but expect a little heat, add a little water to smooth it out or use in the cocktail of your choice.

STRENGTH
50% ABV (100 proof)

MASH BILL
78% corn, 10% rye, 12% malted barley

STILL TYPE
Column still

AGE STATEMENT
10 years

DISTILLERY
Heaven Hill Distillery, Bardstown, Kentucky

BRAND OWNER
Heaven Hill Distillery

PRICE RANGE
$$

DRINKING RECOMMENDATION

In 2004, David and Jane Perkins founded High West Distillery in Park City, Utah, making it the first licensed distillery in the state since the end of Prohibition. Like many start-up distilleries, Perkins began distilling and ageing his own whiskey as well as making a couple of white spirits. To make money while his own whiskey was maturing, he began sourcing and blending whiskeys from Kentucky and Indiana. These blends became immensely popular and as demand grew and supply began to constrict, High West opened a second 2,800 sq m (30,000 sq ft) distillery in Wanship, Utah, to distil and age more of its own whiskey. In 2016, High West was purchased by Constellation Brands for a reported $160 million.

High West Whiskey American Prairie Bourbon
A Blend of Straight Bourbon Whiskeys

STRENGTH
46% ABV (92 proof)

MASH BILL
Undisclosed

STILL TYPE
Column still

AGE STATEMENT
2 years

DISTILLERIES
MGP, Lawrenceburg, Indiana, and undisclosed Kentucky distillery

BRAND OWNER
Constellation Brands

PRICE RANGE
$$

FLAVOUR The nose has a burst of alcohol, followed by baking spices, apple, vanilla and a light note of maraschino cherry. The palate is full-bodied and oak forward with a nice supporting sweetness. On the second sip it is sweeter with more fruit character reminiscent of dried cherries showing through. The bourbon has a long, dry finish, with very light astringency from oak tannins and a touch of fruit. There is a small burn from the alcohol but it is not unpleasant. Neat, this bourbon is likely to appeal to those who like more oak. Use it in a cocktail where you want the wood to balance the sweetness from the other ingredients.

DRINKING RECOMMENDATION

First released in 2012, Hillrock Solera Aged Bourbon was the first bourbon to be matured using the Spanish Solera system of fractional blending. When Hillrock is ready to bottle, a portion of fully matured bourbon is pulled from each barrel but a substantial amount is left in the cask. The pulled bourbon is proofed, bottled and sold. The partially empty old barrels are topped off with bourbon from medium-aged barrels and the medium-aged barrels are topped off with bourbon from young-aged barrels and the young aged barrels are topped off with new-make spirit. Also known as *élevage* (translating as something akin to child-rearing in French), the idea is that the older spirit acts as a tutor and trains up the younger, making it smoother, and allowing it to take on the character of the older spirit.

Hillrock Solera Aged Bourbon Whiskey

FLAVOUR The nose starts with notes of oak, vanilla and dried apple, followed by cloves and a bright note of alcohol but without any harshness. On the palate the bourbon is big and sweet with notes of soft caramel confectionery, raisins and oak, followed up with a hint of milk chocolate. The finish is medium-long with a warm spiciness of cinnamon, balanced with a touch of brown sugar that fades softly with a hint of oak. Overall, this is very well-balanced bourbon that tilts toward the sweet caramel side of the spectrum. While there is some heat from the alcohol, drinking it neat is not overwhelming. It will work well in an Old Fashioned or most bourbon cocktails.

STRENGTH
46.3 ABV (92.6 proof)

MASH BILL
High-rye (37%) mash

STILL TYPE
Column still

AGE STATEMENT
NAS

DISTILLERY
Undisclosed distillery and Hillrock Estate Distillery, Ancram, New York State

BRAND OWNER
Hillrock Estate Distillery

PRICE RANGE
$$$$

DRINKING RECOMMENDATION

Hooker's House Bourbon is named for the home of Civil War general Joseph Hooker, located in Sonoma, California. Created by Fred Groth of Prohibition Spirits, mature barrels of sourced high-rye bourbon are given a second maturation for nine months in Carneros Pinot Noir barrels. Carneros is located at the southern end of the Napa and Sonoma Valleys, right on San Pablo Bay in Northern California. After nine months, the bourbon is vatted and bottled at 100 proof.

Hooker's House Bourbon Sonoma-Style American Bourbon

STRENGTH
50% ABV (100 proof)

MASH BILL
54% corn, 46% rye

STILL TYPE
Column still

AGE STATEMENT
6 years

DISTILLERY
MGP, Lawrenceburg, Indiana

BRAND OWNER
Prohibition Spirits

PRICE RANGE
$$

FLAVOUR The nose on this bourbon is sweet and caramel forward with a touch of red fruit. On the palate the whiskey starts smooth and sweet and then begins to dry out. There is a definite wine flavour that comes through, full of jam and minerality with just a hint of vanilla and spice. The finish is bright with a strong note of oak, followed by raspberry and a hint of bubble gum in the background. It can be enjoyed neat, on the rocks or in a cocktail and will probably be preferred by those looking for a sweeter, less oak-forward bourbon.

DRINKING RECOMMENDATION

Founded in 2003 by Ralph Erenzo and Brian Lee, Tuthilltown Spirits was the first producer of whiskey and bourbon in New York State since the end of Prohibition. Using 100% New York State-grown corn, Tuthilltown mashes, ferments and pot distils the corn whiskey and then ages it for one year in small charred new oak barrels. Because of the smaller barrel, the bourbon is able to draw colour and wood flavours from the cask more quickly than with a standard barrel. After one year, the barrels are vatted and the bourbon is bottled at 92 proof. In 2010, Tuthilltown Spirits was named Distillery of the Year by the American Distilling Institute, and in April 2017, the company was fully purchased by William Grant & Sons, the third-largest producer of Scotch whisky in the United Kingdom.

Hudson Baby Bourbon Whiskey

FLAVOUR The nose has clear notes of vanilla and caramel, followed by rye spice and oak with a hint of sweet cherries. The bourbon is smooth and sweet on the tongue and has a light note of fresh apple. The finish is dominated by oak tannins and has an underlying note of glacé cherries. The bourbon shows great promise for what it could be with more time to mature; however, right now it is fairly young with lots of oak tannins. It will probably interest those who like older oak-forward bourbons because of its wood character. Try drinking it neat or in a Manhattan.

STRENGTH
46% ABV (92 proof)

MASH BILL
100% New York State corn

STILL TYPE
Pot still

AGE STATEMENT
1 year

DISTILLERY
Tuthilltown Spirits, Gardiner, New York State

BRAND OWNER
William Grant & Sons

PRICE RANGE
$$$

DRINKING RECOMMENDATION

The first-ever Iowa Bourbon was released in 2010 by Jeff and Laurie Quint of Cedar Ridge Distillery. After founding the distillery in 2005 Quint was inspired to make bourbon in part because Iowa is one of the USA's leading growers of corn yet none of it was being used in the state to make bourbon. After developing a mash bill featuring Iowa corn, including some farmed by his in-laws, Quint released the first-ever Iowa Bourbon in 2010. Today the whiskey is pot distilled around 180 proof to create what he describes as a smoother flavour, then aged for at least four years and bottled between 80 and 86 proof. The distillery also produces a Reserve Iowa Bourbon that has a five-year age statement and is bottled at 92 proof. In 2017, Cedar Ridge was named Distillery of the Year by the American Distilling Institute.

Iowa Bourbon Whiskey

STRENGTH
43% ABV (86 proof)

MASH BILL
75% corn, 10% rye, 15% malted barley

STILL TYPE
Pot still

AGE STATEMENT
NAS

DISTILLERY
Cedar Ridge Distillery, Swisher, Iowa

BRAND OWNER
Cedar Ridge Distillery

PRICE RANGE
$$

FLAVOUR Caramel and oak meet you on the nose, followed by light notes of vanilla and sweet cherries. The palate starts sweet with flavours of caramel and milk chocolate, then toward the back of the palate oak adds a nice balance but the flavour stays in the background. The finish is long and sweet with a light note of oak and cherries. Overall, this is an enjoyable bourbon that is well balanced and tilts slightly toward sweet and red fruit flavours. It would work well in a sweeter-style Manhattan, and can definitely be drunk neat for those who like a sweet bourbon.

DRINKING RECOMMENDATION

Located in Denison, in the northeast corner of Texas, Ironroot Republic has been slowly gaining recognition for its whiskeys. In 2015, it released Promethean Bourbon, which uses an unusual mash bill made up of 95% corn, including purple corn, yellow corn and two varieties of red corn, rounded out with 5% rye. The whiskey is mashed, fermented and pot distilled, then goes into charred new oak barrels; however, the barrels include American, French and European oak varieties that range in char from light to heavy. This variation in maturation gives Ironroot a wider flavour palate to draw from and create with. To help maintain flavour consistency for each whiskey, batch to batch, expert blender Nancy "The Nose" Fraley picks which barrel in which proportions should go into the bottle.

Ironroot Promethean Bourbon Whiskey

FLAVOUR On the nose there is lots of wood and spice with an underlying fruit character that is common in young corn whiskeys. On the palate, there is plenty of caramel followed by a sweet smoothness. The second sip shows oak coming through with some spice reminiscent of cinnamon candies but without the heat. The finish is dry and oak forward with a bit of wood smoke. As the finish lingers there is a touch of dried fruit that lightens somewhat. This is a good bourbon for those who like lots of oak character. Try drinking it neat or use it in a cocktail to add a dry spiciness to the drink.

STRENGTH
51.5% ABV (103 proof)

MASH BILL
95% corn (includes purple, yellow and two varieties of red corn grown in Texas), 5% rye

STILL TYPE
Pot still

AGE STATEMENT
16 months

DISTILLERY
Ironroot Republic Distilling, Denison, Texas

BRAND OWNER
Ironroot Republic Distilling

PRICE RANGE
$$$

DRINKING RECOMMENDATION

First released in 2016, Ironroot Hubris Corn Whiskey is made from 100% corn, 95% of which is yellow corn grown in Texas and the rest heirloom purple corn. After being distilled, the new-make whiskey goes into used or uncharred barrels for 16 months before being vatted and bottled at 117.8 proof. While the ageing requirement for corn whiskey to use uncharred or used barrels prevents it from legally being classed as bourbon, it makes an interesting contrast to see the difference used cooperage versus new cooperage can make in a whiskey.

Ironroot Hubris Corn Whiskey

STRENGTH
58.9% ABV (117.8 proof)

MASH BILL
95% Texas yellow dent corn, 5% heirloom purple corn

STILL TYPE
Pot still

AGE STATEMENT
16 months

DISTILLERY
Ironroot Republic Distilling, Denison, Texas

BRAND OWNER
Ironroot Republic Distilling

PRICE RANGE
$$$

FLAVOUR The nose has warm wood notes of oak and cedar followed by some spice and a faint touch of vanilla. Initially, the bourbon starts sweet with apple and vanilla flavours before transitioning to seasoned oak with a lot of pepper. With the addition of water the sweet fruity character comes forward and the dry spice dissipates. The finish is hot, short and dry from the alcohol and oak tannins, with flavours of Fuji apple, cinnamon and nutmeg. Neat, the whiskey is hot and spicy with lots of dry oak and hints of sweetness. Therefore, this is probably best drunk with a little water, on the rocks or in a cocktail that needs a sweeter whiskey once diluted.

DRINKING RECOMMENDATION

The Henry family have been farming in Wisconsin for over 71 years and, in 2015, they converted that seven decades of knowledge about the earth and grain into bourbon. While their whiskey is distilled off-site by another distillery, the Henry family grow the grain used for their bourbon and oversee the maturation of the barrels at their farm. Once the whiskey has reached a minimum age of five years they vat the barrels they want, using the services of Nancy "The Nose" Fraley, and bottle their Wisconsin bourbon at 92 proof.

J. Henry & Sons Small Batch Wisconsin Straight Bourbon Whiskey

FLAVOUR The first thing you notice is a strong note of bubble gum followed by some fruitiness. After a little time to breathe, the bourbon begins to show notes of oak and spice. The palate has a creamy texture, which is sweet with a touch of oakiness. In the finish there are lots of oak tannins followed by a hint of spice. This bourbon is unique and may speak to those who like more fruity cocktails. Easy to drink neat, it is probably best suited to those looking for a whiskey that is different from your average Kentucky bourbon.

STRENGTH
46% ABV (92 proof)

MASH BILL
60% heirloom red corn, 14% wheat, 14% rye, 12% malted barley

STILL TYPE
Column still

AGE STATEMENT
5 years

DISTILLERY
Undisclosed Wisconsin distillery

BRAND OWNER
Henry Farms Prairie Spirits

PRICE RANGE
$$$

DRINKING RECOMMENDATION

Jasper Newton "Jack" Daniel was born about 1850 and learned how to distil from a local preacher, Dan Call, and his slave, Nathan Green. In 1875, Daniel and Call built a distillery and started using square bottles in 1897. "Old No.7" stems from the distillery's registration as the seventh distillery in the district. Daniel gave the distillery to two nephews in 1907 and died in 1911. One nephew, Lemuel Motlow, ran the distillery until 1910, when statewide Prohibition was enacted. Motlow, a Tennessee State Senator, helped to repeal Prohibition in 1938 but suspended production in 1942 until 1947. In 1956, the Motlow family sold Jack Daniel's to Brown-Forman, which controls it today. In 1987, the Old No.7 proof dropped from 90 to 86, and then down to 80 in 2002, presumably to allow more whiskey to be bottled.

Jack Daniel's Old No.7 Sour Mash Tennessee Whiskey

STRENGTH
40% ABV (80 proof)

MASH BILL
80% corn, 8% rye, 12% malted barley

STILL TYPE
Column still

AGE STATEMENT
NAS

DISTILLERY
Jack Daniel's Distillery, Lynchburg, Tennessee

BRAND OWNER
Brown-Forman

PRICE RANGE
$$

FLAVOUR Initially dry and slightly hot, this warms to notes of caramel, apricot jam, marzipan and peanut brittle. Over time, this develops to dry notes of sweet tea and charred wood. Like the nose, this is dry, but quickly warms on the palate with light notes of banoffee and crackers. The finish is a tad sweeter, with notes of caramel and vanilla with hints of coffee and maple before a lingering note of oak that is dry and slightly papery. This is a straightforward whiskey that is great in a range of mixed drinks or with cola.

DRINKING RECOMMENDATION

Gentleman Jack was first released in 1988 and was the first Jack Daniel's variant in quite some time. The primary difference between Old No.7 and Gentleman Jack is that the former goes through the Lincoln County Process (filtering the spirit through a tall column of sugar maple charcoal) once before barrelling, while Gentleman Jack gets the Lincoln County Process a second time after the barrels are fully matured. Jack Daniel's claims that this gives Gentleman Jack a more refined character and a smoother finish.

Jack Daniel's Gentleman Jack Tennessee Whiskey

FLAVOUR The bourbon has a mellow, smooth nose with notes of almond, warm spice and fresh straw. On the palate, it is smooth and creamy, with notes of oak, vanilla, cinnamon and a hint of banana. These flavours continue on to the finish, accompanied by light notes of honey and a combination of dry apple and lightly charred wood. This is a smoother, creamier expression of Jack Daniel's that is elegant and more sippable.

STRENGTH
40% ABV (80 proof)

MASH BILL
80% corn, 8% rye, 12% malted barley

STILL TYPE
Column still

AGE STATEMENT
NAS

DISTILLERY
Jack Daniel's Distillery, Lynchburg, Tennessee

BRAND OWNER
Brown-Forman

PRICE RANGE
$$

DRINKING RECOMMENDATION

The 100 Proof edition of Jack Daniel's Single Barrel was originally only released for sale in duty-free stores around the world. However, today it can be found throughout the US and in a number of export markets.

Jack Daniel's Single Barrel Tennessee Whiskey

STRENGTH
50% ABV (100 proof)

MASH BILL
80% corn, 8% rye, 12% malted barley

STILL TYPE
Column still

AGE STATEMENT
NAS

DISTILLERY
Jack Daniel's Distillery, Lynchburg, Tennessee

BRAND OWNER
Brown-Forman

PRICE RANGE
$$$

FLAVOUR The bourbon has a creamy, sweet and indulgent nose full of notes of pecan, dried cherry, peanut brittle and a hint of desiccated coconut. The palate is dry but powerful, with more notes of peanut, pecan and sesame seeds, alongside warm spiced oak, caramel and light banoffee. After a few seconds, this dries out to smoother wood notes that take you on to the finish, where you also find light banana, fragrant wood and touches of dark brown sugar. A warm but elegant whiskey that would be great mixed in classic cocktails or served on the rocks; although full of flavour, it won't ruin your palate.

DRINKING RECOMMENDATION

Frank Sinatra became a huge fan and apostle of Jack Daniel's and according to Nelson Eddy, historian for Jack Daniel's, Sinatra's love of the Old No.7 brand (*see page 106*) and his influence helped grow it into the most popular American whiskey sold in the United States. In commemoration of Sinatra's affinity for its Tennessee whiskey, Jack Daniel's released Sinatra Select as an ultra-premium whiskey in 2013. Instead of new-make spirit going into standard charred new barrels, Sinatra Select is aged in charred new barrels that have deep grooves carved into them, allowing the whiskey more access to the wood.

Jack Daniel's Sinatra Select Tennessee Whiskey

FLAVOUR The nose on this bourbon is soft, warm cinnamon mixed with the sweetness of chocolate and baked apple, with hints of unripe banana and caramel, wrapped up with notes of creamy vanilla and dusty oak. A slight, bright note of peppermint cream appears after a few minutes. The flavour profile starts out with genuine caramel notes that develop into toffee, before turning to more bitter woody notes. There is a prominent, distinctive note of musky wood that dominates the middle of the palate. On top, there are notes of liquorice, dark chocolate and a bitter, organic stalkiness. The finish has a pleasant warmth, along with notes of banana and vanilla, before slightly bitter liquorice root and light tannins. It is flavourful and fun to explore either neat or with ice.

STRENGTH
45% ABV (90 proof)

MASH BILL
80% corn, 8% rye, 12% malted barley

STILL TYPE
Column still

AGE STATEMENT
NAS

DISTILLERY
Jack Daniel's Distillery, Lynchburg, Tennessee

BRAND OWNER
Brown-Forman

PRICE RANGE
$$$$$

DRINKING RECOMMENDATION

Jefferson's Bourbon was first released in 1997, created by Trey Zoeller and his father Chet. In 2005, Jefferson's, which was originally a 100% sourced Kentucky bourbon was purchased by Castle Brands, but in 2015, Castle Brands purchased a 20% share of Kentucky Artisan Distillery. Jefferson's is now said to include sourced bourbon plus some aged bourbon from Kentucky Artisan Distillery.

Jefferson's Very Small Batch Kentucky Straight Bourbon Whiskey

STRENGTH
41.5% ABV (83 proof)

MASH BILL
Undisclosed

STILL TYPE
Column still

AGE STATEMENT
NAS

DISTILLERIES
Kentucky Artisan Distillery, Crestwood, Kentucky and undisclosed Kentucky distillery

BRAND OWNER
Castle Brands

PRICE RANGE
$$

FLAVOUR The nose is bright and fruity with notes of vanilla and baked apple followed by a light hint of oak. On the palate the bourbon has a light body and is semisweet with a note of caramel. The finish is simple and light with gentle oak tannins. Overall, this is a simple, straightforward bourbon with a strong oak character on the finish, which mellows nicely with a little water or in a tall cocktail.

DRINKING RECOMMENDATION

Jefferson's Reserve Bourbon was first released in 1997 and is a mix of 15-year-old bourbon and three other bourbons, each with a separate mash bill and age. It was designed to be a bolder whiskey with more oak character and complexity compared to the regular expression of Jefferson's Bourbon.

Jefferson's Reserve Very Old Kentucky Straight Bourbon Whiskey Very Small Batch

FLAVOUR The nose opens with pleasant aromas of vanilla and caramel, followed by a touch of fresh cherries and red apple. The palate is light and sweet in the mouth, with sweet cherries shining through and just a hint of grain spice toward the back of the palate. The finish is mildly warm, long and semidry, with dominant notes of oak and vanilla. Jefferson's Reserve is a slightly more interesting and richer bourbon than the regular small batch. Because of that, try drinking it neat if you like a little more oak-forward bourbon or drink it with a couple of drops of water to enhance the sweetness.

STRENGTH
45.1% ABV (90.2 proof)

MASH BILL
Undisclosed

STILL TYPE
Column still

AGE STATEMENT
NAS

DISTILLERIES
Kentucky Artisan Distillery, Crestwood, Kentucky and undisclosed Kentucky distillery

BRAND OWNER
Castle Brands

PRICE RANGE
$$

DRINKING RECOMMENDATION

Jefferson's Ocean Bourbon takes mature Kentucky bourbon, about eight years old, and places the barrels on a container ship that crisscrosses the globe – crossing the equator four times – before returning to Kentucky to be dumped. In their time at sea the barrels are in constant motion from the movement of the ship and experience significant temperature fluctuations in addition to breathing in the sea air. These factors combined create a unique environment for maturation that affects the flavour of the whiskey, similar in some ways to finishing the spirit in a second cask, except without using another barrel.

Jefferson's Ocean Aged at Sea Kentucky Straight Bourbon Whiskey Very Small Batch

STRENGTH
45% ABV (90 proof)

MASH BILL
Undisclosed

STILL TYPE
Undisclosed

AGE STATEMENT
NAS

DISTILLERIES
Kentucky Artisan Distillery, Crestwood, Kentucky and undisclosed Kentucky distillery

BRAND OWNER
Castle Brands

PRICE RANGE
$$$$

FLAVOUR The bourbon has a fragrant nose of peach and apricot, with beautiful notes of caramel and buttery pastry and just a touch of cinnamon. On the palate rich notes of cherry liqueur and dark chocolate fade into savoury, herbal notes of black pepper and dark green vegetables – not stewed vegetal notes, but fresh, green leaves like kale and spinach with a hint of salt. The finish returns to sweeter notes of salted caramel and clean wood, with hidden notes of baked peach. This bourbon has excellent complexity – and would be perfect served on its own or perhaps with ice.

DRINKING RECOMMENDATION

Jacob Beam, the son of German immigrants, began selling whiskey in Kentucky in 1795. His son David moved the company to Nelson County, Kentucky and after Prohibition, James Beauregard Beam built a new distillery in Clermont, Kentucky, and created Jim Beam Bourbon. From 1946, Jim's son, T. Jeremiah Beam, grew the business substantially and Master Distiller Booker Noe, grandson of Jim Beam, oversaw the filling of the one millionth barrel of Jim Beam Bourbon in 1965. In 1987, Beam purchased National Distillers, acquiring Old Crow and Old Grand-Dad (*see* pages 138 and 142). Fast forward to 2014, Jim Beam was sold to Suntory Holdings forming Beam Suntory, one of the largest producers of distilled spirits. Today, Jim Beam White Label is the best-selling bourbon in the world.

Jim Beam White Label Kentucky Straight Bourbon Whiskey

FLAVOUR The nose is light and fresh with sweet vanilla, oak and hints of citrus. Soft, sweet caramel fades into a distinct hint of pear drops. In contrast to the nose, the palate is definitely not sweet, with strong, savoury wood notes, hints of straw and a subtle, gradually building warmth accompanied by peppery spice. The finish is smooth, with notes of lightly toasted oak, spice and an echo of the sweet vanilla from the nose. Classic and mellow but with a fine level of spice, this is a versatile bourbon: it is good both on the rocks and in cocktails like the Mint Julep or Old Fashioned.

STRENGTH
40% ABV (80 proof)

MASH BILL
75% corn, 13% rye, 12% malted barley

STILL TYPE
Column still

AGE STATEMENT
NAS

DISTILLERIES
Jim Beam Distilleries, Clermont, Boston and Frankfort, Kentucky

BRAND OWNER
Beam Suntory

PRICE RANGE
$

DRINKING RECOMMENDATION

In 1978, Jim Beam Black Label was introduced as an eight-year-old Kentucky straight bourbon, right at the beginning of bourbon's decline in popularity. However, due in part to the bourbon boom and growing demand for Beam products, the Black Label dropped its age statement in 2015 and now simply states "Extra-Aged".

Jim Beam Black Extra-Aged Kentucky Straight Bourbon Whiskey

STRENGTH
43% ABV (86 proof)

MASH BILL
75% corn, 13% rye, 12% malted barley

STILL TYPE
Column still

AGE STATEMENT
NAS

DISTILLERIES
Jim Beam Distilleries, Clermont, Boston and Frankfort, Kentucky

BRAND OWNER
Beam Suntory

PRICE RANGE
$

FLAVOUR The bourbon has sweet vanilla and caramel notes on the nose and is bright with distinguishable elements of oak toward the end. After a few minutes, hints of milk chocolate develop, too. This whiskey is warming and immediately savoury on the lips, with a textured flavour profile full of notes of oak and vanilla and hints of caramel that are never overly sweet. It has an immensely savoury/dry finish. Good, straightforward and revitalizing with excellent warmth, this bourbon is versatile and mixable in both tall and short cocktails.

DRINKING RECOMMENDATION

First introduced around 2011, Jim Beam Devil's Cut takes bourbon barrels, usually about six years old, dumps them and then "sweats" them, which extracts extra bourbon that has seeped into the wood. This extracted whiskey is very tannic and has a very deep colour. The extracted whiskey is then added back to the vatted bourbon, which gives Devil's Cut a darker colour and more intense wood flavour.

Jim Beam Devil's Cut Kentucky Straight Bourbon Whiskey

FLAVOUR The nose is fruity and woody, with a faint hint of chilli on top of notes of toffee and banana sponge. It is smooth on the palate, with clean, creamy notes of vanilla and oak that gradually warm with hints of peppery spice. The notes of oak continue on to the finish, alongside notes of toasted wood and a little almond. A clean, no-nonsense whiskey that puts oak centre stage and would work well in a wide array of cocktails.

STRENGTH
45% ABV (90 proof)

MASH BILL
75% corn, 13% rye, 12% malted barley

STILL TYPE
Column still

AGE STATEMENT
NAS

DISTILLERIES
Jim Beam Distilleries, Clermont, Boston and Frankfort, Kentucky

BRAND OWNER
Beam Suntory

PRICE RANGE
$$

DRINKING RECOMMENDATION

First released in 2013, Jim Beam Signature Craft Bourbon is a permanent addition to the Jim Beam line-up. Barrels with a minimum age of 12 years are selected from the Jim Beam rickhouses, vatted and proofed down to 43% ABV before being bottled. As well as this expression, Jim Beam also produced a limited edition Signature Craft bourbon that included the addition of a small amount of Spanish brandy.

Jim Beam Signature Craft Kentucky Straight Bourbon Whiskey

STRENGTH
43% ABV (86 proof)

MASH BILL
75% corn, 13% rye, 12% malted barley

STILL TYPE
Column still

AGE STATEMENT
12 years

DISTILLERIES
Jim Beam Distilleries, Clermont, Boston and Frankfort, Kentucky

BRAND OWNER
Beam Suntory

PRICE RANGE
$$

FLAVOUR This bourbon has a honeyed sweetness on the nose, with rich dark sugar and spice notes alongside hints of cherry and herbal cola. To taste, it is powerful and peppery, with distinct notes of black liquorice from the start that gradually develop into sweeter oak flavours. The palate remains creamy but dry throughout. The finish also has notes of black liquorice, accompanied by dashes of treacle, honey and oak, with a hint of black pepper at the end. It is a flavourful bourbon that can be served neat, on the rocks or in a simple cocktail like a Whiskey Sour.

DRINKING RECOMMENDATION

First released on Derby Day in 2013, this is the third expression in the Jim Beam Distiller's Masterpiece line. The current bottling takes extra-aged bourbon and finishes it in Pedro Ximénez sherry casks before bottling it at 100 proof. Compared to other ultra-premium whiskeys, not much detail is provided about this bourbon. As a NAS straight bourbon, it could well be four years old since there is no legal definition for extra-aged. Beam also does not disclose how long the bourbon rests in the sherry casks. At $200 a bottle, producers would usually tend to offer more information as justification for the higher price point, but the company must assume the bourbon does all the talking it needs to.

Jim Beam Distiller's Masterpiece Bourbon Whiskey Finished in PX Sherry Casks

FLAVOUR This bourbon has a rich and complex nose, with an interplay of chocolate, liquorice and treacle alongside freshly polished wood notes. Sweet popcorn flavours follow, like corn-on-the-cob topped with butter and brown sugar. It is powerful on the palate, with rich soaked grain notes and flavours of fresh wood with treacle, brown sugar and a little unripe banana, which makes it slightly reminiscent of a Navy rum. The flavours develop into more raw notes of oak, but the banana and dark sugar notes linger on to the finish. This is a full-bodied whiskey that would be perfect served on the rocks or with a splash of ice-cold mineral water.

STRENGTH
50% ABV (100 proof)

MASH BILL
75% corn, 13% rye, 12% malted barley

STILL TYPE
Column still

AGE STATEMENT
NAS

DISTILLERIES
Jim Beam Distilleries, Clermont, Boston and Frankfort, Kentucky

BRAND OWNER
Beam Suntory

PRICE RANGE
$$$$

DRINKING RECOMMENDATION

Colonel John J. Bowman was a frontiersman who explored Kentucky County, Virginia in the 1770s and later became Sheriff of Lincoln County, Kentucky. After the repeal of Prohibition, A. Smith Bowman, the great, great nephew of Col. Bowman founded the first distillery in Virginia. In 1988, the distillery moved to Spotsylvania County, Virginia and was purchased by Sazerac in 2003. Today John J. Bowman Bourbon begins as a twice distilled new make of Buffalo Trace mash bills #1 and #2. White spirit is shipped from Kentucky to Virginia, and the two-mash bill mix is distilled a third time and then aged. It's a fitting tribute to a man who was both a Virginian and a Kentuckian. Once the barrels of bourbon reach maturity they are individually dumped and the bourbon is reduced in strength to 100 proof before bottling.

John J. Bowman Single Barrel Virginia Straight Bourbon Whiskey

STRENGTH
50% ABV (100 proof)

MASH BILL
Buffalo Trace mash bill #1 (10% or less rye) and #2 (12–15% rye)

STILL TYPE
Column still

AGE STATEMENT
NAS

DISTILLERIES
Buffalo Trace Distillery, Frankfort, Kentucky; A. Smith Bowman Distillery, Fredericksburg, Virginia

BRAND OWNER
Sazerac

PRICE RANGE
$$$

FLAVOUR The nose has sweet notes of toffee apple and vanilla, followed by aromas of oak and fresh cornbread. The palate is smooth with notes of sweet caramel, milk chocolate and brown sugar on the front of the tongue. On the mid- and back palate you get notes of fresh baked bread and oak. The finish has some heat, it is long and dry from the oak tannins and the flavour of cinnamon lingers on your tongue. Overall, this whiskey has deep flavours that complement the fruity notes on the nose. It is a nice bourbon to drink neat or add a couple of drops of water to open it up and tone down the heat.

DRINKING RECOMMENDATION

Johnny Drum Private Stock Bourbon was a sourced bourbon that in 2012 carried a 15-year age statement. In 2016, Private Stock dropped its age statement and while it comes out of the Willett Distillery in Bardstown, Kentucky, it is unclear if any of Willett's distilled bourbon is in the bottle.

Johnny Drum Private Stock Straight Kentucky Bourbon Whiskey

FLAVOUR The nose is pleasant with light floral aromas followed by bright fruit notes like table grapes, all of which is undergirded by vanilla and mixed spice. In the mouth the bourbon is full-bodied, starts sweet and quickly becomes dry from the light oak tannins, followed by notes of tobacco and bread. It closes with a slight mineral character. The finish is long, dry and very oak forward, and dissipates with a hint of sweetness and fresh plum. This is definitely an oak-forward bourbon best suited to those who like more wood character in their bourbon. It would work well in a number of tall drinks or in other cocktails that need more of a dry spirit.

STRENGTH
50.5% ABV (101 proof)

MASH BILL
Undisclosed

STILL TYPE
Column still

AGE STATEMENT
NAS

DISTILLERY
Undisclosed Kentucky distillery

BRAND OWNER
Kentucky Bourbon Distillers

PRICE RANGE
$$

DRINKING RECOMMENDATION

In 1892, Joseph A. Magnus was a spirits rectifier in Cincinnati, Ohio, bottling some 20 brands of whiskey, gin and rum. He was forced to close by statewide Prohibition in 1918 but, in 2015, Joseph Magnus's great-grandson Jimmy Turner and his business partner Brett Thompson re-established the company. Turner called on Dave Scheurich of Woodford Reserve, master blender Nancy "The Nose" Fraley and Richard Wolf of Buffalo Trace to help recreate Magnus's whiskey. Based on a 100-year-old sample, Fraley suspected Magnus had finished his bourbon in sherry barrels, and Turner was able to partially confirm this from an advertisement Magnus placed listing sherry casks for sale with the rest of his rectifying equipment.

Joseph Magnus Straight Bourbon Whiskey

STRENGTH
50% ABV (100 proof)

MASH BILL
Rye mash

STILL TYPE
Column still

AGE STATEMENT
NAS

DISTILLERY
MGP, Lawrenceburg, Indiana

BRAND OWNER
Jos. A. Magnus & Co.

PRICE RANGE
$$$$

FLAVOUR Today Magnus Straight Bourbon is a sourced whiskey comprising old bourbon distilled by MGP, which is then finished in Oloroso sherry, Pedro Ximénez and cognac casks. After this second maturation the bourbon is vatted and bottled at 100 proof. The aroma of this bourbon envelops you with a deep and complex nose of fruit cake, dried fruit, mixed spice, candied orange peel, dark cherries and raisins. The palate starts sweet and then is followed by oak and notes of rum and raisin, sweet orange and cherries. The finish is long and dry with lots of residual fruit notes, followed by tobacco, leather and oak. This is a really fantastic bourbon that is well balanced between fruit and oak. Definitely enjoy it neat or pair it with a fine cigar.

DRINKING RECOMMENDATION

One fine day, master blender Nancy Fraley, an occasional pipe smoker, went searching for a spirit to accompany her smoke while she sat in the backyard of her California home. Not satisfied with any one spirit, she took the idea to Magnus and they gave her the green light to create a bourbon truly fit to pair with a fine cigar or pipe. The result is whiskey made from 11- and 18-year-old MGP bourbons that are finished in Armagnac, sherry and cognac casks, vatted and bottled at 108.7 proof. According to Fraley, the Armagnac barrels provided the missing piece she was looking for and at a higher than average proof the bourbon stands up well to a good smoke.

Joseph Magnus Cigar Blend Bourbon

FLAVOUR Cigar Blend has a great nose with notes of vanilla and caramel followed by bright red fruit aromas and dried plum. The palate is sweet with cherries and plum backed up by some dryness from the alcohol and oak. At the back of the palate, notes of spice and cocoa come through. The finish is hot with a lingering sweetness that contains notes of red fruit and tobacco. Overall, this is a very elegant bourbon to drink neat or with a couple of drops of water, and is designed to be paired with a cigar. The heat from the alcohol and the residual sweetness should balance nicely against the cigar's dry smoke.

STRENGTH
54.35% ABV (108.7 proof)

MASH BILL
Rye mash

STILL TYPE
Column still

AGE STATEMENT
NAS

DISTILLERY
MGP, Lawrenceburg, Indiana

BRAND OWNER
Jos. A. Magnus & Co.

PRICE RANGE
$$$$

DRINKING RECOMMENDATION

Kentucky Vintage Bourbon is a sourced whiskey produced by Kentucky Bourbon Distillers. Since the Willett Distillery has only been open a couple of years (*see* page 179) and the bourbon in this bottle must be at least four years old, it is certain that the whiskey came from somewhere else. After being vatted, the bourbon is bottled at 90 proof.

Kentucky Vintage Straight Kentucky Bourbon Whiskey

STRENGTH
45% ABV (90 proof)

MASH BILL
Undisclosed

STILL TYPE
Column still

AGE STATEMENT
NAS

DISTILLERY
Undisclosed Kentucky distillery

BRAND OWNER
Kentucky Bourbon Distillers

PRICE RANGE
$$

FLAVOUR The bourbon has a rich, sweet nose of genuine caramel, milk chocolate and raisin, with sweet grain and corn behind. There is a little biscotti as the sweetness fades and it becomes drier and more woody. It is increasingly dry and woody on the palate, too, but it keeps an element of the caramel smoothness from the nose. Vibrant spice warms throughout and lingers on to the finish, accompanied by solid wood notes, wood smoke, cherry, almond and lasting notes of cinder toffee. This is a serious whiskey with fun elements of cherry bakewell that would work well in a Manhattan cocktail.

DRINKING RECOMMENDATION

Founded in 2010 by Colin Spoelman and David Haskell, Kings County Distillery was the first distillery to make whiskey in Brooklyn, New York, since Prohibition. From the beginning, Kings County took a different approach, looking for something that spoke to the terroir of New York. Its two-grain mash bill consists of 80% New York-grown organic corn, which is mashed and then fermented in open-top wooden fermenters made from the same cedar as the water tanks that dot the New York skyline. The beer is double pot distilled and then aged. While Kings County originally aged its whiskey in small barrels, it has been gradually sizing up and it shows. In 2016, the American Distilling Institute named Kings County Distillery Distillery of the Year for its high standards, leadership and camaraderie in the craft spirits industry.

Kings County Straight Bourbon Whiskey

FLAVOUR The nose is a pleasant combination of caramel and dry oak followed by dark cherries and chocolate. The bourbon is sweet on the palate with notes of rich caramel, dried fruit and a bright note in the background reminiscent of a light green tea. The finish is medium-long and semidry with a prominent oak character and a touch of dark chocolate. Overall, this is a well-balanced bourbon that is showing great strides from the earlier iterations that were matured in smaller barrels. The combination of Scottish pot stills, open fermenters and ageing in larger barrels has really made it a standout worth looking for. Drink it neat or with a drop of water, or use it in your favourite cocktail.

STRENGTH
45% ABV (90 proof)

MASH BILL
80% New York State organic corn, 20% malted barley

STILL TYPE
Pot still

AGE STATEMENT
2 years

DISTILLERY
Kings County Distillery, Brooklyn, New York

BRAND OWNER
Kings County Distillery

PRICE RANGE
$$$$

DRINKING RECOMMENDATION

In July 2016, Kings County Distillery was one of the first craft distilleries to release a bottled-in-bond bourbon. Made from the same mash bill of New York corn and barley as its straight bourbon (*see* page 123), this edition is aged for four years and bottled from whiskey distilled in one season and bottled at 100 proof.

Kings County Bottled-in-Bond Straight Bourbon Whiskey

STRENGTH
50% ABV (100 proof)

MASH BILL
80% New York State organic corn, 20% malted barley

STILL TYPE
Pot still

AGE STATEMENT
4 years

DISTILLERY
Kings County Distillery, Brooklyn, New York

BRAND OWNER
Kings County Distillery

PRICE RANGE
$$$$

FLAVOUR The nose is very rich and decadent with notes of fig, dried fruit, caramel, vanilla and mixed spice. The bourbon is very smooth with a medium body and is slightly sweet on the palate. There are rich and complex flavours of date, raisins, chocolate, vanilla and caramel, followed by spices like cinnamon and cloves. The finish is long and dry, although there is a sense of sweetness from the lingering flavour of vanilla. It closes with warm spice notes intermixed with oak and tobacco. This is a very complex bourbon that is packed full of flavour. Kings County has come into its own and is no longer dominated by small barrel flavours. Drink it neat to experience all of its flavour and intensity, or add a little water to soften the alcohol slightly. It can also be used to make a great Manhattan or better yet, a Brooklyn.

DRINKING RECOMMENDATION

Kings County Barrel Strength Bourbon is a good example of the quality of spirit coming from this distillery. After the new-make bourbon comes off the still it is legally required to go into the barrel at less than 62.5% ABV (125 proof). Kings County ages its barrels in the upstairs, non-temperature-controlled room of its distillery. As a result, the barrels see lots of heat and humidity in New York's summers and are cold and dry in the wintertime. Because of these conditions, over the course of two to four years, the proof of the bourbon in some barrels will creep up, while others lose alcohol. By the time the barrels are pulled and vatted, the bourbon can range from 115 to 128 proof.

KINGS COUNTY DISTILLERY
barrel strength
straight bourbon whiskey
64 % alcohol by volume, 200ml

Kings County Barrel Strength Straight Bourbon Whiskey

FLAVOUR At barrel strength the bourbon has a somewhat closed nose but there are notes of caramel, spice and a touch of oak. With a little bit of water, fruit notes open up. The palate starts sweet and then transitions to show more oak and a note of dark chocolate. Again, with water the flavour opens up and reveals more fruit and flavours reminiscent of scones and honey. On its own the finish is hot, very dry and medium-long, with lingering flavours of vanilla, caramel and a bright sweetness like red wine. With water more fruity notes such as ripe persimmon open up. Neat, it is very intense, so it is probably best drunk with a little water or on the rocks. Overall, this is a powerhouse bourbon that hides its youth and is just really good stuff.

STRENGTH
64% ABV (128 proof)

MASH BILL
80% New York State organic corn, 20% malted barley

STILL TYPE
Pot still

AGE STATEMENT
2 years

DISTILLERY
Kings County Distillery, Brooklyn, New York

BRAND OWNER
Kings County Distillery

PRICE RANGE
$$$

DRINKING RECOMMENDATION

The Peated Bourbon from Kings County Distillery was the result of a happy accident. It so happened that while the distillery was prepping a new batch of grain for the bourbon mash, it ran out of malted barley. However, it happened to have on hand some peated malt so this was added to the mash. The results turned out quite well so Kings County decided to keep this as a regular product in its line-up.

Kings County Peated Bourbon Whiskey

STRENGTH
45% ABV (90 proof)

MASH BILL
70% New York State organic corn, 15% malted barley, 15% peated malt

STILL TYPE
Pot still

AGE STATEMENT
1 year

DISTILLERY
Kings County Distillery, Brooklyn, New York

BRAND OWNER
Kings County Distillery

PRICE RANGE
$$$$

FLAVOUR For this bourbon the nose is fairly sweet with notes of vanilla and a touch of underlying oak for support. As it breathes there are faint hints of ash and caramel. The palate is very sweet with notes of vanilla and caramel, which are balanced nicely against a slightly briny character that is followed by the flavour of fresh cookies. The finish is long, soft and dry, with wood notes and a very light smoke sensation. This is a very nice bourbon, but whatever peat is used seems to show up just minimally in the profile, then stronger on the finish. This is not an Islay lover's bourbon but a solid whiskey with a slightly smoky finish. Overall, it is excellent for such a young bourbon and should be drunk neat.

DRINKING RECOMMENDATION

Knob Creek was originally a straight bourbon produced after Prohibition in Cincinnati, Ohio, at the Penn-Maryland Corporation, which was owned by National Distillers. Beam acquired the Knob Creek brand in 1987 when it purchased National Distillers. The brand remained dormant until it was relaunched in 1992 as part of the Jim Beam Small Batch Collection (*see also* pages 52 and 53). Originally bottled as a nine-year-old 100 proof bourbon, the whiskey became a NAS straight bourbon in 2016 due to high demand and growing popularity. The regular expression of Knob Creek is joined by a 120 proof, nine-year-old Single Barrel Reserve Kentucky Straight Bourbon and a 100 proof Straight Rye Whiskey.

Knob Creek Kentucky Straight Bourbon Whiskey

FLAVOUR At first whiff there is a strong note of alcohol, followed by very light aromas of caramel and vanilla with just a hint of fruit in the background. On the palate the bourbon is full-bodied and has a sweet caramel flavour with light notes of apple and pear combined with oak. On the finish the whiskey is hot but not astringent. The bourbon has a long oak finish, which is somewhat dry from the tannins. After sitting on the tongue, a tobacco note starts to come through. Try drinking this bourbon on the rocks or in a cocktail. It would work particularly well in an Old Fashioned or a Manhattan.

STRENGTH
50% ABV (100 proof)

MASH BILL
75% corn, 13% rye, 12% malted barley

STILL TYPE
Column still

AGE STATEMENT
NAS

DISTILLERIES
Jim Beam Distilleries, Clermont, Boston and Frankfort, Kentucky

BRAND OWNER
Beam Suntory

PRICE RANGE
$$

DRINKING RECOMMENDATION

John E. Fitzgerald, whom this bourbon is named after, was a US Treasury Agent who apparently had a knack for picking good barrels of whiskey. Pre-Prohibition, Charles Herbst created the Old Fitzgerald bourbon brand in honour of the famed tax man and distilled it at the Old Judge Distillery outside Frankfort, Kentucky. In 1999, Heaven Hill acquired the Old Fitzgerald brand and began bottling it from wheated bourbon made at its Bernheim Distillery. Heaven Hill introduced Larceny as a premium version of Old Fitz, made from small batches of about 200 barrels that have aged between six and twelve years.

Larceny Kentucky Straight Bourbon Whiskey Very Special Small Batch

STRENGTH
46% ABV (92 proof)

MASH BILL
68% corn, 20% wheat, 12% malted barley

STILL TYPE
Column still

AGE STATEMENT
NAS

DISTILLERY
Heaven Hill Distillery, Bardstown, Kentucky

BRAND OWNER
Heaven Hill Distillery

PRICE RANGE
$$

FLAVOUR Larceny has a strong woody aroma of oak and cedar, with notes of tobacco, leather and sweet cherries carried up on the alcohol. The flavour has lots of spicy nutmeg and clove notes, with hints of orange candy and milk chocolate. This is a very woody bourbon with strong bitter tannins and a warmth that starts in the mouth and travels down your chest. The finish is long and dominated by wood and spice notes with a slight tinge of heat from the alcohol. If you like your whiskeys more on the woody side of the spectrum this would be a solid purchase. It would be good in a Manhattan that emphasizes the mixed spice and wood notes over sweet cherry.

DRINKING RECOMMENDATION

The Maker's Mark Distillery was founded by Bill and Margie Samuels in 1953. In 1975, Bill Samuels, Sr turned the reins of the company over to his son Bill, Jr, who is credited with transforming Maker's Mark into an internationally recognized brand. During the 1980s, Maker's Mark was sold a few times, although the family maintained control of production. In 2005, the brand became part of the Beam portfolio of bourbons. After 36 years of leading Maker's Mark, Bill Samuels, Jr retired in 2011 and his son Rob Samuels was promoted to the role of Chief Operating Officer.

Maker's Mark Kentucky Straight Bourbon Whisky

FLAVOUR The nose is light and sweet with notes of golden syrup and light brown sugar, but nonetheless has some power behind it. There are also hints of corn and oak and, after a few minutes in the glass, sweeter notes of spiced honey develop. The palate is refreshingly dry and woody, with a lasting warmth and notes of vanilla, butterscotch and toasted oak. The finish is warming and long, focused on oak and spice. It has a classic bourbon profile with a sweet nose and oak-focused palate, and is good to enjoy with ice or in a classic cocktail.

STRENGTH
45% ABV (90 proof)

MASH BILL
70% corn, 16% red winter wheat, 14% malted barley

STILL TYPE
Column still

AGE STATEMENT
NAS

DISTILLERY
Maker's Mark Distillery, Loretto, Kentucky

BRAND OWNER
Beam Suntory

PRICE RANGE
$$

DRINKING RECOMMENDATION

The Maker's Mark Distillery has its founder, Margie Samuels, to thank for its distinctive wax-dipped neck. Margie founded the company with Bill Samuels, Sr, a sixth-generation distiller. She showed a keen eye for design and marketing from the start. While Bill distilled the bourbon and managed the barrels, Margie designed the Maker's Mark bottle and the font for the label and came up with the idea to dip the neck in red wax as well as the Maker's logo. In recognition for her contributions she was inducted into the Kentucky Bourbon Hall of Fame in 2014.

Maker's 46 Kentucky Bourbon Whisky Barrel Finished with Oak Staves

STRENGTH
47% ABV (94 proof)

MASH BILL
70% corn, 16% red winter wheat, 14% malted barley

STILL TYPE
Column still

AGE STATEMENT
NAS

DISTILLERY
Maker's Mark Distillery, Loretto, Kentucky

BRAND OWNER
Beam Suntory

PRICE RANGE
$$

FLAVOUR The nose is very nice – the alcohol is clearly present and carries strong notes of vanilla and oak, with lighter sweet aromas of caramel and burnt wood and a hint of grain or baked bread. As the bourbon sits, the nose opens up with notes of oily tobacco, cedar and cloves. At first sip it is very hot and astringent. With the addition of water aromas of green oak open up, the astringency lightens and cinnamon, cloves and a light sweetness come forward. Neat, the finish is intense and bitter. With a little water this softens and some sweetness hangs on to the tip of the tongue. This bourbon is likely to appeal to those that like the regular Maker's Mark (*see* page 129) and those who like extra-aged bourbon with more oak character at a higher proof. It would work well mixed with soda water or cola, its intensity standing up well to dilution and some added sugar.

DRINKING RECOMMENDATION

First released in 1968 by Seagram, Benchmark Bourbon was positioned initially as a premium whiskey. Then in 1989, Sazerac purchased Benchmark along with Eagle Rare (*see* page 75). Subsequently, Sazerac expanded the name to McAfee's Benchmark Bourbon, which refers to brothers James, Robert, George and Samuel McAfee who surveyed 23 tracts of land around Frankfort, Kentucky, in 1773 and 1775, near the current location of the Buffalo Trace Distillery. Today, this once premium bourbon has been downgraded to a value bourbon, made from the Buffalo Trace mash bill #1 and aged for three years before being bottled at 80 proof.

McAfee's Benchmark Old No. 8 Brand Kentucky Straight Bourbon Whiskey

FLAVOUR The bourbon opens with a light and pleasant aroma. There are notes of oak, cooked corn and spice. After it has had time to breathe, notes of baked apple and a hint of cinnamon open up, followed by aromas of toffee apple and toffee. The palate is smooth, full-bodied and sweet, with notes of toffee balanced with oak tannins and spice character from the rye. There is also a slightly fruity note, somewhere between dried figs and prunes. As the bourbon warms the chest going down, the finish is short and semidry. Overall, the bourbon is clean, with lingering notes of oak and pine. This is a pretty nice bourbon for only three years old.

STRENGTH
40% ABV (80 proof)

MASH BILL
Buffalo Trace mash bill #1 (10% or less rye)

STILL TYPE
Column still

AGE STATEMENT
3 years

DISTILLERY
Buffalo Trace Distillery, Frankfort, Kentucky

BRAND OWNER
Sazerac

PRICE RANGE
$

DRINKING RECOMMENDATION

Michter's began in Pennsylvania in 1753 when Swiss Mennonite farmers John and Michael Shenk created the Shenk Distillery. By 1950, and after a number of name and ownership changes, the distillery, still in Pennsylvania, began making Michter's Original Sour Mash Whiskey. The name "Michter" came from the names of then owner Lou Forman's sons Michael and Peter. After closing in 1989, Mitcher's abandoned trademarks were claimed by Joseph Magliocco and Richard Newman who began sourcing whiskey, bourbon and rye from Kentucky. In late 2014 constricted supply and growing demand led to the installation of an 81cm (32 inch) diameter column still and doubler at Mitcher's plant in Shively, where it is currently bottling sourced whiskey and distilling and maturing its own whiskey for the future.

Michter's Small Batch US*1 Kentucky Straight Bourbon Whiskey

STRENGTH
45.7% ABV (91.4 proof)

MASH BILL
79% corn, 11% rye, 10% malted barley

STILL TYPE
Column still

AGE STATEMENT
NAS

DISTILLERIES
Undisclosed Kentucky distillery; Michter's Distillery, Shively, Kentucky

BRAND OWNER
Chatham Imports

PRICE RANGE
$$

FLAVOUR The nose has a distinct note of alcohol that carries up aromas of vanilla, mint, light oak, apple and cinnamon. The palate is smooth with sweet flavours of unfiltered (cloudy) apple juice, vanilla, oak and cinnamon. The finish is medium-long and semisweet, with notes of toasted oak and dried apple. This is a lovely bourbon to drink neat and on the rocks or use in cocktails.

DRINKING RECOMMENDATION

At the turn of the 20th century, Murray Hill Club blended whiskey was a very popular brand that was sourced, blended and bottled by Jos. A. Magnus & Co. in Cincinnati, Ohio. Due to the passage of statewide Prohibition in 1918, Magnus was forced to shut his doors. Nearly 100 years later, Magnus's great grandson resurrected the company (*see* page 120) and it now sources and blends whiskey in Washington D.C. Today, Murray Hill Club is a blended bourbon that combines 11- and 18-year-old bourbon with 9-year-old light whiskey that is distilled to more than 160 proof and stored in used or uncharred new oak containers. Once the barrels of bourbon and light whiskey are vatted, this blend is bottled at 103 proof.

Murray Hill Club Bourbon Whiskey A Blend

FLAVOUR The bourbon has a wonderful nose: sweet and inviting with notes of caramel, rich dried fruit and vanilla. The palate is sweet with flavours of dried fruit, dark cherries and a touch of vanilla, all balanced nicely with oak. The finish is long and very well balanced between sweet and dry. There is just a touch of heat at the back of the throat but it dissipates quickly. Meanwhile, oak tannins continue to hold on but they have more of a savoury character like toasted seaweed. While this is not a straight bourbon, it is quite delicious and well worth the price of entry if you are looking for a rich, full-flavoured and balanced bourbon to enjoy neat in the evenings.

STRENGTH
51.5% ABV (103 proof)

MASH BILL
Rye mash

STILL TYPE
Column still

AGE STATEMENT
NAS

DISTILLERY
MGP, Lawrenceburg, Indiana

BRAND OWNER
Jos. A. Magnus & Co.

PRICE RANGE
$$$$

DRINKING RECOMMENDATION

In 2006, Andy and Charlie Nelson went with their father Bill to a butcher in Greenbrier, Tennessee. Across from the butcher was an old warehouse and a historical marker telling the story of how Charles Nelson, Andy and Charlie's great-great-great grandfather, built a distillery there and made some of the most popular Tennessee whiskey in the state. From that their passion was ignited and in 2009 they reopened Nelson's Green Brier Distillery. In 2017, they released Nelson's First 108 Tennessee Whiskey, commemorating the 108-year closure period. For this limited release, the brothers distilled the family's wheated whiskey recipe, mellowed it with sugar maple charcoal and aged it in 108 113.5 litre (30 gallon) barrels, before finishing in 200 litre (53 gallon) barrels, vatted and bottling at 90.4 proof.

Nelson's First 108 Sour Mash Tennessee Whiskey

STRENGTH
45.2% ABV (90.4 proof)

MASH BILL
Wheated mash

STILL TYPE
Pot still

AGE STATEMENT
NAS

DISTILLERY
Nelson's Green Brier Distillery, Nashville, Tennessee

BRAND OWNER
Nelson's Green Brier Distillery

PRICE RANGE
$$

FLAVOUR The nose is incredibly complex with notes of caramel, raisins, prunes and tobacco, followed by a wonderful aroma of rich black earth and brown sugar. The palate is smooth and rich, with notes of burnt sugar, vanilla, nutmeg and cocoa, closing with a touch of oak tannins. The finish is medium-long and sweet, with notes of vanilla and caramel intermingled with tobacco and a hint of oak. This is a complex and interesting Tennessee whiskey that shows incredible promise for the whiskeys that are likely to come from Nelson's Green Brier. Drink it neat or in a very special cocktail.

DRINKING RECOMMENDATION

Like its green label brother (*see* page 134), this gold label, single barrel bottling of Nelson's First 108 Tennessee Whiskey is a limited edition to commemorate the fact that the Nelson family are once again distilling and selling whiskey after a 108-year break. After the 108 barrels are all tapped, the whiskey will be gone but these special bottles give an exciting preview of the excellent Tennessee whiskey yet to come from Nelson's Green Brier.

Nelson's First 108 Single Barrel Sour Mash Tennessee Whiskey

FLAVOUR The nose has a pleasant aroma of caramel and apple mixed with green notes of chillies and wood. The bourbon is sweet and full-bodied, with notes of apple and oak and just a hint of vanilla. The finish is smooth, medium-long and dry, with notes of oak, apple and walnuts. Overall, this is a bright, wood-forward bourbon that is incredibly smooth for over 60% ABV. This single barrel bourbon shows a little more youth than the green label First 108 whiskey from Nelson's and shows great promise. Drink it neat, on the rocks or in your favourite cocktail.

STRENGTH
60.5% ABV (121 proof)

MASH BILL
Wheated mash

STILL TYPE
Pot still

AGE STATEMENT
NAS

DISTILLERY
Nelson's Green Brier Distillery, Nashville, Tennessee

BRAND OWNER
Nelson's Green Brier Distillery

PRICE RANGE
$$$

DRINKING RECOMMENDATION

Noah's Mill Bourbon is a sourced bourbon produced by Kentucky Bourbon Distillers (KBD) in Bardstown, Kentucky. KBD has not disclosed who or where the bourbon came from, but it is a non-age-statement bourbon bottled at 114.3 proof.

Noah's Mill Genuine Bourbon Whiskey

STRENGTH
57.15% ABV (114.3 proof)

MASH BILL
Undisclosed

STILL TYPE
Column still

AGE STATEMENT
NAS

DISTILLERY
Undisclosed Kentucky distillery

BRAND OWNER
Kentucky Bourbon Distillers

PRICE RANGE
$$$

FLAVOUR Right up front there is a lot of alcohol on the nose, followed by bright notes of fresh apples, cherries, vanilla and cinnamon supported by oak. The palate has a umami character combined with sweetness and oak. Really well balanced, the flavours are rounded out with notes of cinnamon, cloves, honey and brown sugar. The finish is warm in the mouth – which is not surprising for the proof – is dry and has lots of oak character. As the oak fades you are left with a residual sweetness of cherries. This bourbon leans toward the oak side of the spectrum but it is also likely to be pleasant for those who also like sweeter bourbons. Drink it neat or with a little water, and it would probably make a very nice Manhattan.

DRINKING RECOMMENDATION

According to Willett Distillery, Old Bardstown was first released in the 1940s. Today, Old Bardstown Estate Bourbon is a sourced whiskey bottled by Kentucky Bourbon Distillers. In 2004, Old Bardstown Estate carried a ten-year age statement; however, that was dropped in 2009, although it is still bottled at 101 proof. Willett reopened its distillery in 2012 (*see* page 179), and in 2017 it released an Old Bardstown Bottled-in-Bond Bourbon from four-year-old Willett bourbon. This could mean that the Estate Bottled expression will eventually revert to Willett distilled whiskey instead of sourced bourbon.

Old Bardstown Estate Bottled Kentucky Straight Bourbon Whiskey

FLAVOUR The nose has deep notes of brown sugar and caramel followed by a touch of vanilla and oak. The palate is soft and rich with notes of plum, cherries and vanilla and some sweetness, which is nicely balanced with oak that adds depth and a touch of dryness. The finish is dry and long, with notes of fruit balanced against oak. However, there is no astringency or bitterness. This is a really nice classic bourbon that is a tad on the sweeter side. Drink it neat to experience all of the full flavours or with a little splash of water if you find the alcohol too intense. It will also work well in cocktails that need a sweeter spirit.

STRENGTH
50.5% ABV (101 proof)

MASH BILL
Undisclosed

STILL TYPE
Column still

AGE STATEMENT
NAS

DISTILLERY
Undisclosed Kentucky distillery

BRAND OWNER
Kentucky Bourbon Distillers

PRICE RANGE
$$

DRINKING RECOMMENDATION

In the mid-1800s, Dr James Crow worked as the head distiller at the Oscar Pepper Distillery (now Woodford Reserve Distillery, *see* page 184). Dr Crow was instrumental in modernizing the bourbon industry (*see* page 15) and the resulting Old Crow Bourbon was one of the first branded bourbons sold. After Prohibition, Old Crow was the best-selling bourbon in the USA but by the early 1980s it had fallen from grace, partly due to a change in its production. In 1987, Old Crow was sold to Jim Beam as part of its purchase of National Distillers and for the most part it has remained a bottom-shelf value bourbon. This is a shame given its importance in bourbon history. However, in 2010, Beam released an Old Crow variant called Old Crow Reserve, which is a four-year-old Kentucky straight bourbon bottled at 86 proof.

Old Crow Sour Mash Kentucky Straight Bourbon

STRENGTH
40% ABV (80 proof)

MASH BILL
75% corn, 13% rye, 12% malted barley

STILL TYPE
Column still

AGE STATEMENT
3 years

DISTILLERIES
Jim Beam Distilleries, Clermont, Boston and Frankfort, Kentucky

BRAND OWNER
Beam Suntory

PRICE RANGE
$

FLAVOUR On the nose there are aromas of baked apple, apple boiled sweets and not much else. The palate has a light body and again notes of apple come through, with a touch of caramel and mixed spice. The finish is long and medium-dry on the palate, with flavours of apple, green tea and hibiscus. Old Crow is a nice, light-flavoured bourbon with only a little heat and would be best used in short or tall cocktails.

DRINKING RECOMMENDATION

Created in 1870 by George Garvin Brown and his half-brother John Thompson Street Brown, Jr, Old Forester Bourbon is renowned for being the first sold in sealed glass bottles and during Prohibition was allowed to be sold as "medicinal whiskey". This makes Old Forester the longest-selling bourbon brand in the world. By 1902, when he purchased the Ben Mattingly Distillery in St. Mary, Kentucky to produce his own bourbon, George Brown was the sole owner of Brown-Forman. When production resumed after World War II Brown-Forman purchased its own cooperage to produce bourbon barrels, making it the only major distillery that makes its own barrels. The Old Forester Signature Bourbon is bottled at 100 proof and is joined by seven other expressions, including the Classic (86 proof), 1920 Prohibition Style, Birthday Bourbon and Statesman.

Old Forester Signature Kentucky Straight Bourbon Whiskey

FLAVOUR Bright aromas of fruit and cream, reminiscent of strawberry shortcake or bubble gum, greet your nose at the beginning. As the bourbon breathes a little, vanilla and a very light aroma of oak lie underneath. The palate is warm and sweet on the tip of the tongue, followed by oak. Fruit flavours like nectarines mix with a sweet and full-bodied note of milk chocolate to round things out. The finish is dry with lingering notes of oak and nectarines. Overall, this is a very nice bourbon with a bright and fruity character and is great value for making cocktails.

STRENGTH
50% ABV (100 proof)

MASH BILL
72% corn, 18% rye, 10% malted barley

STILL TYPE
Column still

AGE STATEMENT
NAS

DISTILLERY
Brown-Forman Distillery, Shively, Kentucky

BRAND OWNER
Brown-Forman

PRICE RANGE
$$

DRINKING RECOMMENDATION

First released in 2015, Old Forester 1870 Original Batch Bourbon was created to commemorate the founding of J.T.S. Brown & Bro., the forerunner of the Brown-Forman Company in 1870. George Brown and his half-brother originally purchased straight bourbon from the three distilleries owned by the J.M. Atherton Co. and bottled it as Old Forester Bourbon. Today, the 1870 Original Batch is made by vatting "select barrels" from three Brown-Forman warehouses, with "each barrel originating from a different day of production, with a different entry proof and a different age".

Old Forester 1870 Original Batch Kentucky Straight Bourbon Whisky

STRENGTH
45% ABV (90 proof)

MASH BILL
72% corn, 18% rye, 10% malted barley

STILL TYPE
Column still

AGE STATEMENT
NAS

DISTILLERY
Brown-Forman Distillery, Shively, Kentucky

BRAND OWNER
Brown-Forman

PRICE RANGE
$$

FLAVOUR Alcohol immediately flies up from the glass, but on second inspection notes of vanilla, well-cured oak and dried fruit appear underneath. The palate has a light and mellow sweetness that is well balanced with dryness from the oak and it has a nice flavour of dried cherries. On the finish the bourbon is warm on the tongue but without harshness. There are lingering notes that are lightly sweet and while the oak character persists it is not overpowering. This is not an ostentatious bourbon – it is very well integrated and supremely balanced. It is a great introductory bourbon that you can drink neat or in a cocktail.

DRINKING RECOMMENDATION

First released in 2015, Old Forester 1897 Bottled-in-Bond Bourbon was created to commemorate the passage of the 1897 Bottled-in-Bond Act. This was the first consumer protection law passed in the United States and it required that for a whiskey to be labelled "bottled-in-bond" it must be the product of one distillation season, of one distiller, from one distillery, aged for no less than four years and bottled at exactly 100 proof (*see also* page 40).

Old Forester 1897 Bottled-in-Bond Kentucky Straight Bourbon Whisky

FLAVOUR The nose has notes of vanilla, tobacco, oak and baked apple, with pleasant spice aromas from the barrel and a touch of sweetness. As the bourbon breathes, notes of stone fruit and brown sugar begin to come forward. On the palate there are notes of brown sugar and sarsaparilla, followed by dryness from the oak tannins. The finish is semisweet, with lingering flavours of vanilla and nectarines. Overall, this is a solid go-to bourbon for those that like more oak character than, say, Old Forester 1870 (*see* page 140). It can be drunk neat, on the rocks or in a cocktail where you want to add a bit of dryness and structure.

STRENGTH
50% ABV (100 proof)

MASH BILL
72% corn, 18% rye, 10% malted barley

STILL TYPE
Column still

AGE STATEMENT
NAS

DISTILLERY
Brown-Forman Distillery, Shively, Kentucky

BRAND OWNER
Brown-Forman

PRICE RANGE
$$$

DRINKING RECOMMENDATION

In the late 19th century, Raymond Hayden, the grandson of Basil Hayden (*see* page 53), opened a distillery named Old Grand-Dad in his honour. When Raymond died, the distillery and Old Grand-Dad Bourbon were sold to the Wathen family, who were, like Basil, Kentucky Catholics from the migration from Maryland after the American Revolution. The Wathens sold Old Grand-Dad as "medicinal whiskey" during Prohibition and the brand was acquired by National Distillers shortly thereafter. In 1987, the James B. Beam Distilling Company purchased National Distillers, with Old Grand-Dad Bourbon and its recipe. In addition to the 80 proof expression, Old Grand-Dad is also sold as a bottled-in-bond and at 114 proof.

Old Grand-Dad Kentucky Straight Bourbon Whiskey

STRENGTH
40% ABV (80 proof)

MASH BILL
63% corn, 27% rye, 10% malted barley

STILL TYPE
Column still

AGE STATEMENT
NAS

DISTILLERIES
Jim Beam Distilleries, Clermont, Boston and Frankfort, Kentucky

BRAND OWNER
Beam Suntory

PRICE RANGE
$

FLAVOUR Soft, slightly musky, but comforting vanilla and the light sweetness of caramel. Notes of dried wheat, oatmeal and soft, toasted grain fade into wood notes with a hint of milk-chocolate-dipped strawberries and tarter raspberry. To taste, this has a soft but not lightweight texture. Dry and refreshing wood notes come to the fore – younger green wood notes to start, which develop into notes of aged oak – with vanilla and a dash of caramel. The finish is also surprisingly dry, with notes of English breakfast tea, dark chocolate and peach stones, with occasional bursts of vanilla from the nose. It is perfect served neat, without ice or water, or lengthened in a Highball with chilled soda water.

DRINKING RECOMMENDATION

Old Grand-Dad Bourbon contains about twice as much rye as the standard Jim Beam mash bill. And historically, Old Grand-Dad Bonded Bourbon has been the #1 selling bottled-in-bond bourbon in the United States. In 2015, Beam Suntory redesigned the Old Grand-Dad label and raised the price by $5.

Old Grand-Dad Bonded Kentucky Straight Bourbon Whiskey

FLAVOUR This bourbon has a rich, textured nose with a full-bodied sweetness reminiscent of maple syrup on top of fruity notes of cherry and chocolate-covered strawberries. This is followed by chewy, puffed rice and a little raisin, before cleaner notes of polished wood and rye. It is warm on the palate, with a complex flavour that slowly develops. It starts out with dry but fruity notes of grain, with cherry and dry notes of soda water that fade into green notes of herbal cola. Toward the finish, rich oak notes take on a more creamy texture with hints of grape. The finish has notes of grains, raisins and honey. Savoury chocolate notes fade into dry oak, with hints of black pepper. It is a complex bourbon that is full of flavour, perfect served neat or on the rocks.

STRENGTH
50% ABV (100 proof)

MASH BILL
63% corn, 27% rye, 10% malted barley

STILL TYPE
Column still

AGE STATEMENT
NAS

DISTILLERIES
Jim Beam Distilleries, Clermont, Boston and Frankfort, Kentucky

BRAND OWNER
Beam Suntory

PRICE RANGE
$$

DRINKING RECOMMENDATION

Founded by Brad Irwin in 2007, Oregon Spirit Distillers began production in 2009. It makes a variety of spirits, including whiskey, gin and absinthe, from grain to glass. Irwin is proud of the fact that the company is able to use all Oregon-grown grains in the production of its spirits. In 2013, Oregon Spirit Distillers released its first straight whiskey, C.W. Irwin Bourbon. However, in 2017, it phased out production of C.W. Irwin and introduced its Straight American Bourbon. Irwin's ultimate goal for his bourbon is for it to show balance between the grain and the oak.

Oregon Spirit Distillers Straight American Bourbon Whiskey

STRENGTH
47% ABV (94 proof)

MASH BILL
Four-grain mash

STILL TYPE
Pot still

AGE STATEMENT
4 years

DISTILLERY
Oregon Spirit Distillers, Bend, Oregon

BRAND OWNER
Oregon Spirit Distillers

PRICE RANGE
$$

FLAVOUR The first thing that comes to your nose is the aroma of cornbread, followed by light floral notes intermixed with sweet aromas like ripe cherries, vanilla and sweet tea. All of this is undergirded by pleasant aromas of oak. The palate is dark and rich, with absolutely zero heat in the mouth. The bourbon tastes of dried fruits like raisins and prunes, followed by vanilla and oak. There is a slight sensation of tannins, which give the impression of a balanced sweetened tea. The finish is long and dry with some heat that quickly dissipates. Notes of oak and grain persist with just a hint of ripe peach. This is a really nice four-year-old bourbon that would work well on the rocks or in a cocktail such as a Manhattan or eggnog.

DRINKING RECOMMENDATION

One of a growing number of craft distillers to release a bottled-in-bond bourbon, Oregon Spirit Distillers ferment its four-grain mash, distil it twice in a pot still and then let it age for four years. Once the barrels are mature, they are vatted and the whiskey is reduced in strength to 100 proof.

Oregon Spirit Distillers Bottled-in-Bond Bourbon Whiskey

FLAVOUR The nose opens with rich notes of caramel and cinnamon underlain with oak. As the whiskey breathes, notes of leather and cured tobacco appear, followed by a hint of sweet cornbread. The palate starts sweet and transitions to being dry. With a little heat on the tongue, the bourbon is full-bodied and has a very grain-forward taste of fresh corn and is slightly vegetal, followed by light bitter tannins from the oak. There are hints of fresh fruit like white peaches. The finish has some heat that lingers and bright notes of fresh oak, fresh baked bread and tobacco. Overall, this bourbon has a fantastic aroma, but it is a little disappointing in the palate, although the finish is nice. It should show well on the rocks or in a variety of cocktails.

STRENGTH
50% ABV (100 proof)

MASH BILL
Four-grain mash

STILL TYPE
Pot still

AGE STATEMENT
4 years

DISTILLERY
Oregon Spirit Distillers, Bend, Oregon

BRAND OWNER
Oregon Spirit Distillers

PRICE RANGE
$$

DRINKING RECOMMENDATION

Outlaw Bourbon, from Yellow Rose Distilling owners Ryan Baird, Troy Smith and Randy Whitaker, began production in 2012, two years after the distillery was founded outside Houston, Texas. Outlaw Bourbon is unusual in that it is made from 100% Texas-grown corn, which is then pot distilled. After distillation, the new-make whiskey is aged for six months in 38 litre (10 gallon) barrels before being vatted and bottled at 92 proof. Between the small barrels and the Texas climate, Outlaw Bourbon picks up a lot of colour in a very short period of time.

Outlaw Bourbon Whiskey

STRENGTH
46% ABV (92 proof)

MASH BILL
100% corn

STILL TYPE
Pot still

AGE STATEMENT
6 months

DISTILLERY
Yellow Rose Distilling,
Pinehurst, Texas

BRAND OWNER
Yellow Rose Distilling

PRICE RANGE
$$$

FLAVOUR The nose is very fruity with a sweet aroma of apple and a hint of bubble gum. The palate starts sweet with notes of vanilla and apple and then begins to dry out with a big wallop of spice. The finish is long and semisweet, with flavours of oak and mixed spice. This is a surprisingly good bourbon for its youth. It also demonstrates the complexity that can come from a 100% corn whiskey, pot distilled and aged in intense conditions. Drink it neat if you like spicy or oak-forward bourbons; it also works in a number of cocktails.

DRINKING RECOMMENDATION

Julian P. Van Winkle and Alex Farnsley purchased a controlling interest in W. L. Weller & Sons (*see* page 168) in 1896. During Prohibition, Van Winkle secured a licence to sell "medicinal whiskey". In 1933 Van Winkle merged with one of its primary suppliers to form the Stitzel-Weller Distillery, which sold a wheated bourbon under the Old Fitzgerald and Weller bourbon brands. From 1992 Diageo, the current owners of Stitzel-Weller, have used the distillery only for ageing spirits and so the old wheated bourbon brands were sold off. Meanwhile, Julian, Jr formed the Old Rip Van Winkle company, bottling whiskey from its kept-back aged stock. In 2002, the family entered into a partnership with Buffalo Trace who distills, ages and bottles five expressions of Van Winkle Bourbon, including a 10-year-old whiskey bottled at 107 proof.

Pappy Van Winkle's Family Reserve Kentucky Straight Bourbon Whiskey 15 Years Old

FLAVOUR The nose of the Family Reserve is very light with notes of bright unfiltered (cloudy) apple juice, cinnamon and a touch of caramel. However, on the palate the bourbon has a rich, sweet entry that dries quickly. There are some very nice floral notes followed by red fruit and plum. At 107 proof there is some heat on the tongue, which is not unexpected. With a couple of drops of water the alcohol calms down and pleasant spice notes open up. The finish is long and oak forward, with a touch of vanilla and fruit. This is quite nice for ageing 15 years in a new oak barrel. Like the other Pappy editions, it is fairly oak forward but not overwhelmingly so, which is a testament to the barrel selection and vatting of Pappy. Drink it neat if you like your bourbon on the aggressive side or add a little water to open it up a little.

STRENGTH
53.5% ABV (107 proof)

MASH BILL
Buffalo Trace wheated mash (16–18% wheat)

STILL TYPE
Column still

AGE STATEMENT
15 years

DISTILLERY
Buffalo Trace Distillery, Frankfort, Kentucky

BRAND OWNER
Old Rip Van Winkle Distillery

PRICE RANGE
$$$$

DRINKING RECOMMENDATION

The 20-year-old Family Reserve bourbon is the second oldest in the Van Winkle line-up and it is bottled at 90.4 proof. One of the reasons a bourbon like this is so expensive is because each year some percentage of a barrel of whiskey evaporates. This evaporation is referred to as the angel's share. Multiply that by 20 years and you may only end up with 75 litres (20 gallons) of whiskey from a once full 200 litre (53 gallon) barrel. The second reason is the increase in demand. More people are seeking this bourbon out, which drives prices up. Most liquor stores in the US have started holding lotteries to see who will get the right to purchase one bottle.

Pappy Van Winkle's Family Reserve Kentucky Straight Bourbon Whiskey 20 Years Old

STRENGTH
45.2% ABV (90.4 proof)

MASH BILL
Buffalo Trace wheated mash (16–18% wheat)

STILL TYPE
Column still

AGE STATEMENT
20 years

DISTILLERY
Buffalo Trace Distillery, Frankfort, Kentucky

BRAND OWNER
Old Rip Van Winkle Distillery

PRICE RANGE
$$$$$

FLAVOUR The bourbon opens with a bright and fruity nose of apple and pear, followed by a hint of vanilla and some underlying oak and spice. As the whiskey breathes, notes of caramel and dates begin to come through. The palate starts sweet and moves to semidry. Surprisingly, it has a light body and taste of apple and pears, with a nice note of cinnamon and sweet cherries. The finish is long and dry, with notes of vanilla, fruit and oak. Pappy 20 is the best of the lot and an excellent example of extra-aged bourbon. This is definitely an oak-forward bourbon that should be drunk neat and savoured.

DRINKING RECOMMENDATION

The 23-year-old Family Reserve is currently tied with Elijah Craig 23 (*see* page 79) for being the oldest regular production bottlings of bourbon available in the market. Pappy 23 is a testament to the fantastic barrel management of Buffalo Trace and the Van Winkle family. While many bourbons at 15 and 20 years would end up tasting like you were chewing on a stick, some very special barrels have what it takes to go the distance. What the factors are that make one barrel at Buffalo Trace over-oaked at 12 years and a second barrel divine at 23 are not precisely known. That being said, warehouse placement and tannin levels in the wood are probably part of the answer.

Pappy Van Winkle's Family Reserve Kentucky Straight Bourbon Whiskey 23 Years Old

FLAVOUR The nose is inviting. It starts light and develops into deep notes of vanilla, caramel, pear and sweet cherries, with only the slightest hint of alcohol. Initially, the bourbon is a bit hot on the palate and the flavours open with lots of oak and sweet vanilla. However, this sweetness is balanced well by the oak and some soft notes of mixed spice. The finish lingers with notes of vanilla and dried fruit, and overall it is very dry from lots of oak. This is an incredibly oak-forward bourbon, with some additional pleasant flavours, and is definitely one for those who love lots of oak in their whiskey. Drink it neat or with a couple of drops of water to tame the alcohol and slightly calm the oak intensity.

STRENGTH
47.8% ABV (95.6 proof)

MASH BILL
Buffalo Trace wheated mash (16–18% wheat)

STILL TYPE
Column still

AGE STATEMENT
23 years

DISTILLERY
Buffalo Trace Distillery, Frankfort, Kentucky

BRAND OWNER
Old Rip Van Winkle Distillery

PRICE RANGE
$$$$$

DRINKING RECOMMENDATION

Dave Thibodeau, Bill Graham and Rory Donovan founded Peach Street Distillers in 2005 in Palisade, Colorado. Since its beginning, Peach Street has focused on producing fruit and grain spirits from the local crops grown in and around Palisade. Its bourbon is made from a rye mash that includes Colorado-grown corn. After fermenting in an open-air container, the distiller's beer is distilled once in a hybrid pot–column still that allows it to get up to the proof required in one pass. The new-make spirit is then barrelled for two to five years. Once the bourbon reaches maturity, the barrels are vatted and it is bottled at 92 proof. In 2012, Peach Street Distillers was named Distillery of the Year by the American Distilling Institute.

Peach Street Colorado Straight Bourbon Whiskey

STRENGTH
46% ABV (92 proof)

MASH BILL
60% Colorado corn, 20% rye, 20% malted barley

STILL TYPE
Pot–column still

AGE STATEMENT
2 years

DISTILLERY
Peach Street Distillers, Palisade, Colorado

BRAND OWNER
Peach Street Distillers

PRICE RANGE
$$$

FLAVOUR Youthful and very grain forward, the nose smells of fresh baked cornbread. It also has a light fruitiness resembling green table grapes balanced with oak. The palate is smooth and tastes sweet, with notes of unfiltered (cloudy) apple juice and caramel, followed by cinnamon and some grain character. The finish has more notes of grain and oak followed by a hint of sweetness. The finish is smooth and semidry with zero heat. There is a hint of fruit that I can't put my finger on, followed by unfiltered (cloudy) apple juice and cinnamon. This is a very nice fruit-forward bourbon that is reminiscent of apple brandy. Drink it neat or use it in a bourbon cocktail or a cocktail that calls for apple brandy.

DRINKING RECOMMENDATION

First released exclusively in the southern United States in 1961, Rebel Yell was created by Charlie Farnsley, one-time mayor of Louisville, Kentucky, in 1948 as a private label bourbon. However, Rebel Yell ended up as a wheated bourbon produced at the Stitzel-Weller Distillery in Shively, Kentucky. When public demand for bourbon began to slip, the distillery and its brands were sold in 1972 and eventually wound up in the hands of Diageo (*see page 147*). In 1999, Diageo sold Rebel Yell to Luxco, based in St. Louis, Missouri, and it began sourcing wheated bourbon to use in its whiskey, staying true to its heritage. Initially, Luxco was open about the fact it sourced its bourbon from Heaven Hill Distillery but it will no longer confirm that. Today, Rebel Yell is a value bourbon that's at least four years old and bottled at 80 proof.

Rebel Yell Kentucky Straight Bourbon Whiskey

FLAVOUR A bright nose of slightly oxidized green apples is followed by buttery pastry, making this reminiscent of tart apple pie. As it warms, these notes are accompanied by more subtle hints of caramelized sugar and rich vanilla custard. On the palate, tart and dry notes of apple continue, developing into slightly but not unpleasantly astringent notes of wood. These flavours continue on to the finish, which is dry and tart. A clean but dry whiskey that would go marvellously with sweeter mixers such as ginger ale, or in cocktails.

STRENGTH
40% ABV (80 proof)

MASH BILL
Wheated mash

STILL TYPE
Column stil

AGE STATEMENT
NAS

DISTILLERY
Undisclosed Kentucky distillery

BRAND OWNER
Undisclosed Kentucky distillery

PRICE RANGE
$

DRINKING RECOMMENDATION

In 2008, Luxco released the first bottling of Rebel Yell Small Batch Reserve Bourbon. Unfortunately, it does not provide any additional information about what makes the Small Batch Reserve different from the regular expression of Rebel Yell (*see* page 151) other than it is bottled at a higher proof. Presumably, the reserve bourbon is made from slightly older barrels of wheated bourbon – but that is not explicitly stated, it is merely implied.

Rebel Yell Small Batch Reserve
Kentucky Straight Bourbon Whiskey

STRENGTH
45% ABV (90 proof)

MASH BILL
Wheated mash

STILL TYPE
Column still

AGE STATEMENT
NAS

DISTILLERY
Undisclosed Kentucky distillery

BRAND OWNER
Luxco

PRICE RANGE
$$

FLAVOUR The bourbon has almond and marzipan on the nose, with notes of custard, creamy oatmeal and a hint of maple. The oat notes continue on to the palate, which warms gently with hints of light brown sugar. It gradually becomes drier, with oak, a grassy stalkiness and a creamy nuttiness. The finish is lovely and dry, with clean wood shavings and a hint of dark chocolate. It would work well in a Manhattan with a dash of maraschino.

DRINKING RECOMMENDATION

Founded in 2010 by Phil Brandon, Rock Town Distillery produces a number of whiskeys, vodka, gin, rum and a liqueur. Its Rock Town Bourbon is made with Arkansas-grown corn and soft red winter wheat, as well as some malted barley brought in from out of state. This wheated mash is pot distilled and matured for at least 12 months – according to Brandon the average is between 14 and 16 months – in small charred new oak barrels made by a local Arkansas cooper. Once the bourbon is mature, it is vatted and bottled without chill filtering at 92 proof.

Rock Town Arkansas Bourbon Whiskey

FLAVOUR Sweet naan bread with a honeyed sweetness on the nose, it is doughy with notes of yeast, vanilla and oak. On the palate, this is powerful and textured from the outset and grows increasingly dry with a bite of yeasty flavours. It quickly becomes spicy and particularly savoury with notes of black pepper. These linger on to the finish, accompanied by faint hints of cherry and dark chocolate, before a neutral, dry note of hay.

STRENGTH
46% ABV (92 proof)

MASH BILL
82% Arkansas corn, 9% Arkansas soft red winter wheat, 9% malted barley

STILL TYPE
Pot still

AGE STATEMENT
12 months

DISTILLERY
Rock Town Distillery, Little Rock, Arkansas

BRAND OWNER
Rock Town Distillery

PRICE RANGE
$$

DRINKING RECOMMENDATION

John Rowan was an early settler in Kentucky who moved with his family from Pennsylvania to the area around Bardstown, Kentucky. Rowan studied the law and served in a number of political and elected positions in Kentucky and Washington D.C. Rowan's Creek, named after John Rowan, is a stream that runs through the grounds of the Willett Distillery (*see* page 179) and from which the bourbon takes its name. Like some of the other bourbons from the Kentucky Bourbon Distillers, Rowan's Creek Bourbon is a sourced NAS whiskey bottled at 100.1 proof. In the past, Rowan's Creek carried a 12-year age statement; however, that has now been dropped, meaning the bourbon is a minimum of four years old.

Rowan's Creek Straight Kentucky Bourbon Whiskey

STRENGTH
50.05% ABV (100.1 proof)

MASH BILL
Undisclosed

STILL TYPE
Column still

AGE STATEMENT
NAS

DISTILLERY
Undisclosed Kentucky distillery

BRAND OWNER
Kentucky Bourbon Distillers

PRICE RANGE
$$

FLAVOUR The nose is very nice with notes of burnt sugar, apple and pear. The palate has a fruity flavour resembling unfiltered (cloudy) apple juice, but with a nice balance of oak and vanilla. The finish is light and fruity and very well balanced between sweetness and the dryness from the alcohol and oak. Overall, this is a very pleasant bourbon that can be sipped neat; alternatively, add a couple of drops of water to calm the alcohol down. It would also work well in cocktails that need a more fruity bourbon.

DRINKING RECOMMENDATION

First released in 2001, Russell's Reserve Bourbon – a 10-year-old edition of Wild Turkey bottled at 90 proof – was created as a collaboration between Jimmy and Eddie Russell (*see* page 175) and is a reflection of the way Jimmy likes his bourbon. It serves as a testament to the dedication and skill the Russell family have demonstrated in making some of the finest American whiskey over the past 60 years.

Russell's Reserve Kentucky Straight Bourbon Whiskey 10 Years Old

FLAVOUR The nose has notes of butterscotch with soft warm aromas of oak logs burning, ripe pears and light tannins. The palate is silky-smooth with very light heat and notes of sweet vanilla that are balanced with oak and tobacco. The bourbon has a slightly fruity character reminiscent of some brandies and has a long finish with notes of oak and bright Chardonnay. Russell's Reserve is an excellent bourbon that is a delight to drink – it is the epitome of a well-balanced bourbon and very impressive for a 10-year-old, 90 proof bourbon. Most bourbons of this age, I find, are over-oaked, but this is a great testament to the Russell legacy.

STRENGTH
45% ABV (90 proof)

MASH BILL
75% corn, 13% rye, 12% malted barley

STILL TYPE
Column still

AGE STATEMENT
10 years

DISTILLERY
Wild Turkey Distillery, Lawrenceburg, Kentucky

BRAND OWNER
Gruppo Campari

PRICE RANGE
$$

DRINKING RECOMMENDATION

Smooth Ambler's Old Scout Bourbon was first released in 2011. While Smooth Ambler opened its doors in 2010, John Little and company decided to create a line of sourced whiskeys while their own was maturing. They began purchasing barrels of whiskey from MGP; once the barrels are fully mature, they are vatted and bottled at 99 proof.

Smooth Ambler Old Scout Straight Bourbon Whiskey

STRENGTH
49.5% ABV (99 proof)

MASH BILL
60% corn, 36% rye, 4% malted barley

STILL TYPE
Column still

AGE STATEMENT
6 or 7 years depending on the bottling

DISTILLERY
MGP, Lawrenceburg, Indiana

BRAND OWNER
Pernod Ricard

PRICE RANGE
$$

FLAVOUR A light, bright nose of maple syrup drizzled over cherries and strawberries, followed by freshly polished wood and creamier notes of marzipan, amaretti and meringue. The cherry notes grow richer with time to notes of raisin and cinnamon. On the palate, there are bright notes of wood that sweeten slightly with notes of syrup, honey and fruit. Creamy oak follows, before a long, dry, creamy finish, with fruity berry notes on top reminiscent of red vermouth. The oak notes build along with the distinctive dryness of dark chocolate and hints of wafer. A bright, vibrant bourbon that is full of flavour.

DRINKING RECOMMENDATION

Similar to the regular expression of Old Scout Bourbon (*see* page 156), Old Scout Ten Bourbon is a sourced bourbon from MGP; however, there is a larger proportion of corn in the mash bill compared to the seven-year-old Old Scout. Once the whiskey has reached maturity, the barrels are vatted and bottled at 100 proof.

Smooth Ambler Old Scout Ten Straight Bourbon Whiskey 10 Years Old

FLAVOUR A darker nose than the seven-year-old edition, with more raisin, a touch of molasses and charred wood added to a base of cherries, amaretti and a little crème caramel. This whiskey has a complex and constantly developing flavour profile. A salinity kicks off at the start, reminiscent of salted caramel. This develops into clean notes of oak and caramel with a light grassiness and even a subtle charred wood note. Just before the finish, a fruitiness unfurls with notes of cherry and raspberry. The finish is of dry, creamy and substantial oak, with occasional flashes of spice and berry notes. A darker, spicier whiskey than the seven-year-old Old Scout, but equally complex and fun to explore neat.

STRENGTH
50% ABV (100 proof)

MASH BILL
75% corn, 21% rye, 4% malted barley

STILL TYPE
Column still

AGE STATEMENT
10 years

DISTILLERY
MGP, Lawrenceburg, Indiana

BRAND OWNER
Pernod Ricard

PRICE RANGE
$$$

DRINKING RECOMMENDATION

Smooth Ambler Contradiction, a blended straight bourbon, is a mixture of two bourbons made from different mash bills. One is distilled from a wheated mash at Smooth Ambler and aged for at least two years, while the second is a nine-year-old bourbon distilled from a high-rye mash by MGP of Lawrenceburg, Indiana. When each bourbon has reached maturity, the whiskey is vatted and bottled at 100 proof.

Smooth Ambler Contradiction A Blend of Straight Bourbon Whiskies

STRENGTH
50% ABV (100 proof)

MASH BILL
Mix of 60% corn, 20% wheat, 20% malted barley and 75% corn, 21% rye, 4% malted barley

STILL TYPE
Column still

AGE STATEMENT
NAS

DISTILLERIES
MGP, Lawrenceburg, Indiana and Smooth Ambler Spirits, Maxwelton, West Virginia

BRAND OWNER
Pernod Ricard

PRICE RANGE
$$$

FLAVOUR Contradiction has a sweet, spicy nose: toffee and creamy vanilla fudge drawing out to more of a woody dryness, accompanied by notes of sweet tea, a little pineapple and apricot jam. The nose settles to notes of oak and pineapple cubes. On the palate, this is dry, but vibrant. Powerful and peppery, it has a warming but lasting flavour of black peppercorns and a little chilli. Over time, this develops to dry, creamy notes of oak with notes of raisins and granola. The finish is pleasantly dry, with notes of oak and fudge and richer hints of brandy-soaked Christmas pudding and blackcurrant jelly. Overall, the bourbon has an interesting and long-lasting flavour profile with great intensity of flavour. It is perfect served neat or on the rocks to fully appreciate the range of flavours.

DRINKING RECOMMENDATION

First released in 2017, this is not a sourced bourbon but rather Smooth Ambler's own spirit distilled from a wheated mash and matured for five years before being vatted and bottled at 100 proof. First distilled in 2012, the release of the distillery's own straight bourbon has been much anticipated due in part to the large following it has amassed from its Old Scout line (*see* pages 156–7). If you pick up a bottle of this wheated bourbon, know that it is pot distilled in West Virginia rather than the column-distilled rye bourbon from MGP used for Old Scout.

Smooth Ambler Wheated Bourbon Straight Bourbon Whiskey

FLAVOUR This bourbon has a comforting nose of wheat, bran and corn, with the soft, musky sweetness of honey and golden syrup. On the palate, the wheat comes through; the flavour profile is spiced and dry, with occasional bursts of sweetness. The finish is very dry, with wood notes intermingled with leather and dried orange peel. The wheat comes through again at the end of the finish.

STRENGTH
50% ABV (100 proof)

MASH BILL
Most probably 73% corn, 15% wheat, 12% malted barley

STILL TYPE
Pot still

AGE STATEMENT
NAS

DISTILLERY
Smooth Ambler Spirits, Maxwelton, West Virginia

BRAND OWNER
Pernod Ricard

PRICE RANGE
$$$

DRINKING RECOMMENDATION

Around 2014, the Stein family released their first batch of five-year-old straight bourbon made in Joseph, Oregon. It is pot distilled from a two-grain mash of family-grown corn and barley. The new-make spirit is aged for five years, then vatted and bottled at 80 proof. In 2014, the Stein Distillery also began providing its five-year-old bourbon for Black Maple Hill Bourbon, a brand that once bottled a wheated bourbon distilled at the famed Stitzel-Weller Distillery in Kentucky, but as demand for well-aged bourbon grew, Black Maple Hill's owner CVI had to find a new supply.

Stein Distillery Small Batch Straight Bourbon Whiskey Aged 5 Years

STRENGTH
40% ABV (80 proof)

MASH BILL
75% corn, 25% malted barley

STILL TYPE
Pot still

AGE STATEMENT
5 years

DISTILLERY
Stein Distillery, Joseph, Oregon

BRAND OWNER
Stein Distillery

PRICE RANGE
$$

FLAVOUR The nose is nice and sweet with caramel, followed by green notes of grain and oak. There is also a hint of fresh cherries and red apples. The palate has lots of caramel and vanilla with light fruit notes of plum and peach, supported by young oak. The finish is long, soft and semisweet, with notes of green apple, caramel, chocolate and oak tannins. Overall, this is a nice oak-forward bourbon that has light fruit notes and a balanced sweetness. Drink it neat or in a fruity cocktail.

DRINKING RECOMMENDATION

Owner James Fowler opened Sugar House Distillery in Salt Lake City, Utah, in 2014 and almost immediately began distilling vodka and malt whiskey. In 2015, Sugar House laid down its first barrels of bourbon, which had been pot distilled from a mash of Utah-grown corn, rye and malted barley. After the whiskey has matured for about a year, the barrels are vatted and the bourbon is bottled at 86 proof. As a craft distiller, Fowler is proud of the fact that Sugar House is involved at every step in the process, from fermentation to packaging.

Sugar House Distillery Bourbon Whiskey

FLAVOUR Soft caramel notes come up from the glass, followed by notes of bubble gum, wood and cinnamon. The palate is a sweet, smooth and medium-bodied bourbon, which has a light flavour of caramel, cloves, bubble gum and oak. The finish is slightly warm, with a medium-long and dry finish that has flavours of caramel spice and young oak. This is a dry, oak-forward young whiskey that is enjoyable and will probably be preferred by those who like wood-forward and spicy bourbons. Drink it neat, on the rocks or in a cocktail.

STRENGTH
43% ABV (86 proof)

MASH BILL
Rye mash

STILL TYPE
Pot still

AGE STATEMENT
1 year

DISTILLERY
Sugar House Distillery, Salt Lake City, Utah

BRAND OWNER
Sugar House Distillery

PRICE RANGE
$$

DRINKING RECOMMENDATION

Founded by Guy and Tanya Endsley, Fire Oak Distillery is a new craft distillery located in Liberty Hill, Texas, just 56km (35 miles) northwest of Austin. Fuelled by a passion for fine spirits, Endsley has struck out to make not only a bourbon in Texas, but also a Texas bourbon that is bold, full of flavour and with a little southwestern spice. The distillery's bourbon, first released in 2017, is made from a high-rye mash and pot distilled. The new-make spirit is then put into barrels for a minimum of two years before it is vatted and bottled at 90 proof.

Texas Bourbon Small Batch Whiskey

STRENGTH
45% ABV (90 proof)

MASH BILL
High-rye (20% or more) mash

STILL TYPE
Pot still

AGE STATEMENT
2 years

DISTILLERY
Fire Oak Distillery, Liberty Hill, Texas

BRAND OWNER
Fire Oak Distillery

PRICE RANGE
$$

FLAVOUR The nose has a bright note of green oak balanced with a deep earthy aroma – resembling a thick underlayer of leaves beneath an oak tree – that is slightly sweet with a hint of brown sugar. The palate is sweet and full-bodied with notes of caramel and mixed spice. The finish is medium-warm and starts bright and sweet, then fades into a light, dry note of oak and ends with a strong spice character. While the nose has an unusual earthiness to it, the rest of the drinking experience is very enjoyable. Although the bourbon still shows some signs of youth it also has a good balance between sweetness and oak. Despite the more oaky side of the finish, this bourbon would appeal to a broad section of bourbon drinkers. Drink it neat or use it in your favourite cocktail.

DRINKING RECOMMENDATION

Tom Herbruck opened Tom's Foolery Distillery in 2011 and released his first straight bourbon in 2014. Two years later, Tom was able to release one of the first-ever bottled-in-bond craft bourbons. Tom's Foolery Bonded Bourbon is pot distilled and, according to David Driscoll, the Assistant Head Buyer of wine and spirits for California's famed K&L Wines, the whiskey is sometimes a mixture of both wheated and rye bourbon mash bills that have aged for a minimum of four years. Once matured, barrels laid down in the same season are vatted and the bourbon is bottled at 100 proof.

Tom's Foolery Bonded Bourbon
Ohio Straight Bourbon Whiskey

FLAVOUR The nose is full of grain and oak aromas, followed by a light note of baked apple. The palate is viscous, and smooth, with a flavour that is well balanced between sweetness and oak with a slightly floral character. While the finish has some heat, it starts semisweet, followed by notes of oak, grain and dry tannins. The finish is interesting because it is both slightly briny and floral, with a fleeting sense of magnolia. This is a grain- and oak-forward bourbon that should be drunk with a little water for those who like woody whiskey, or use it in a cocktail that needs a dry whiskey.

STRENGTH
50% ABV (100 proof)

MASH BILL
Varies

STILL TYPE
Pot still

AGE STATEMENT
4 years

DISTILLERY
Tom's Foolery Distillery, Chagrin Falls, Ohio

BRAND OWNER
Tom's Foolery Distillery

PRICE RANGE
$$$

DRINKING RECOMMENDATION

Founded in 2010 by Leonard Firestone and Troy Robertson, Firestone & Robertson Distilling Co. makes unique Texas bourbon. With the skill of head distiller Rob Arnold, they propagated a wild yeast strain that could fully ferment their mash and produce a flavour profile they liked. In a stroke of luck, they found their wild yeast on a pecan nut, which comes from the state tree of Texas. The team create a mash of Texas-grown No. 2 yellow dent corn, Texas soft red winter wheat and six-row malted barley, and ferment it with their "Brazos" domesticated yeast strain. The mash, grain and all, is distilled to barrel proof using a hybrid pot–column still and the new-make spirit is matured for at least four years. First released in January 2017, TX Texas Straight Bourbon is currently a little over four years old and bottled at 90 proof.

TX Texas Straight Bourbon Whiskey

STRENGTH
45% ABV (90 proof)

MASH BILL
Wheated mash

STILL TYPE
Pot–column still

AGE STATEMENT
NAS

DISTILLERY
Firestone & Robertson Distilling Co., Fort Worth, Texas

BRAND OWNER
Firestone & Robertson Distilling Co.

PRICE RANGE
$$

FLAVOUR The nose is very fragrant with notes of vanilla and dried fruit, followed by aromas of baked bread and fresh apple, with an underlying oak character that adds structure. The palate starts sweet with notes of caramel and apple, which is well balanced with flavours of oak and pepper spice. The finish is warm, semisweet and long, with notes of oak and spice, with a hint of dark plum. Overall, this is a spicy, semisweet bourbon with a healthy dose of oak. It will probably be most popular with those who like an oak-forward bourbon with a touch of sweetness. Drink it neat or use it in your favourite cocktail.

DRINKING RECOMMENDATION

Daric Schlesselman founded Van Brunt Stillhouse in 2012 and, in addition to rum, grappa and moonshine, Schlesselman makes a few whiskeys. The Van Brunt name comes from a Dutch farmer and possible distiller who lived in what became Brooklyn, New York. The whiskey is pot distilled from a four-grain mash of New York-grown corn, rye, wheat and malted barley. The new-make spirit is matured in small barrels for at least one year. When the whiskey reaches maturity, it is vatted and bottled at 84 proof.

Van Brunt Stillhouse Bourbon Whiskey

FLAVOUR The nose is very woody with notes of cedar, green oak and acorns, followed by aromas of light pear cider and green wheat. The bourbon is smooth with a medium body that is semisweet. The light caramel flavour is quickly overwhelmed by wood and a flavour of fresh corn husks. The finish is slightly warm and long, with notes of chocolate and a green wood flavour that is slightly bitter. This is a young whiskey aged in small barrels that give it a very strong flavour of green wood. While the spirit shows signs that it is distilled very well, maturing the whiskey in small barrels in the extreme high and low temperatures of Brooklyn results in the extraction of a ton of oak tannins and bitter flavours. This whiskey might appeal to those who like very wood-forward bourbons or very hoppy lagers. It would be best used in a cocktail or with cola.

STRENGTH
42% ABV (84 proof)

MASH BILL
65% corn, 20% wheat, 5% rye, 10% malted barley

STILL TYPE
Pot still

AGE STATEMENT
1 year

DISTILLERY
Van Brunt Stillhouse, Brooklyn, New York

BRAND OWNER
Van Brunt Stillhouse

PRICE RANGE
$$$

DRINKING RECOMMENDATION

Located in Seattle's Capitol Hill, OOLA Distillery was founded in 2010 by Kirby Kallas-Lewis. Waitsburg Bourbon was originally a mixture of small-cask-aged OOLA and sourced bourbon but Waitsburg has now transitioned to 100% OOLA whiskey. A mash of corn, rye, barley and wheat is pot distilled and barrelled. While 85–90% of the bourbon goes into full-sized charred new oak barrels for five years, the remaining 10–15% goes into 57 litre (15 gallon) barrels stored in the warm mezzanine above the still room, then in the evening cool marine air is pumped in to cool them down. The barrels remain for up to two years before being transferred to full-sized barrels to finish their five years of maturation. Once the bourbon reaches maturity, it is vatted and bottled at 94 proof.

Waitsburg Bourbon Whiskey

STRENGTH
47% ABV (94 proof)

MASH BILL
Four-grain mash

STILL TYPE
Pot still

AGE STATEMENT
NAS

DISTILLERY
OOLA Distillery, Seattle, Washington

BRAND OWNER
OOLA Distillery

PRICE RANGE
$$

FLAVOUR The alcohol carries up bright and pleasant notes of vanilla and caramel apple, followed by mixed spice. The palate is soft and has a full umami character, with notes of tobacco, oak, burnt sugar and a slight saltiness. The finish is smooth and long, with notes of tobacco, dried apricots and deep wood flavours with a slight touch of bitterness. Overall, the bourbon is really interesting and is much more savoury than a standard bourbon. Drink it neat or use it in a cocktail where you want to tone down the sweetness of the other ingredients.

DRINKING RECOMMENDATION

In addition to its 94 proof expression of Waitsburg Bourbon (*see* page 166), OOLA also produces a cask-strength edition. Made in the same way as its regular bourbon, the cask-strength version is about five years old and bottled at 116 proof.

Waitsburg Cask Strength Bourbon Whiskey

FLAVOUR This aromatic bourbon has fragrant and rich notes of cinnamon and nutmeg, followed by sweet aromas of crème brûlée and rum and raisin. The palate is sweet and full-bodied, with big flavours of baking spices, vanilla and caramel and a touch of oak for balance. The finish is long, semidry and warm, with notes of rum and raisin, dates, vanilla and caramel. Overall, this is a big sweet bourbon that is completely drinkable at 58% ABV and definitely a whiskey for those who like sweeter bourbons. Drink it neat or add a little water if it is too hot; it would also work well in cocktails that need a sweeter bourbon.

STRENGTH
58% ABV (116 proof)

MASH BILL
Four-grain mash

STILL TYPE
Pot still

AGE STATEMENT
NAS

DISTILLERY
OOLA Distillery, Seattle, Washington

BRAND OWNER
OOLA Distillery

PRICE RANGE
$$$

DRINKING RECOMMENDATION

In 1849, William Larue Weller created a wholesale liquor business called W. L. Weller & Sons, producing Old W. L. Weller, Mammoth Cave and Cabin Still bourbons from sourced whiskey. In 1896, Julian Van Winkle and Alex Farnsley purchased Weller's controlling shares after his retirement and, in 1933, Van Winkle, Farnsley and Arthur Stitzel merged the Weller and A. Ph. Stitzel companies into a single entity: the Stitzel-Weller Distillery (see page 147), eventually owned by Diageo. In 1999, Diageo sold the Weller brand to Sazerac who expanded it to four expressions all made from the Buffalo Trace wheated mash bill. Weller Special Reserve used to be affordable, but now allocation has made it rare and much more expensive. Sazerac also bottles a barrel-proof expression that is part of its Antique Collection (see page 94), William Larue Weller.

Weller Special Reserve Kentucky Straight Bourbon Whiskey

STRENGTH
45% ABV (90 proof)

MASH BILL
Buffalo Trace wheated mash (16–18% wheat)

STILL TYPE
Column still

AGE STATEMENT
NAS

DISTILLERY
Buffalo Trace Distillery, Frankfort, Kentucky

BRAND OWNER
Sazerac

PRICE RANGE
$$

FLAVOUR The nose is pleasingly light, with notes of vanilla and sweet orange, followed by cherries and a note of alcohol. The palate has a nice balance of oak and sweetness, with notes of vanilla and caramel followed by cinnamon spice, and a very soft mouthfeel that is really pleasant. The finish is soft and semidry, with notes of oak and stone fruit. This is an excellent bourbon – drink it neat or on the rocks, or use it to make an outstanding cocktail.

DRINKING RECOMMENDATION

Weller Antique, also known as Old Weller Antique, was originally introduced as Weller Original Barrel Proof sometime after the repeal of Prohibition in the United States. At the time, it was a common practice among Kentucky bourbon distillers to put the new-make spirit into the barrel at 107 proof. It is common in Kentucky that as a spirit matures, its angel's share (evaporation from the barrel) will be mostly water, causing the proof to rise over time, which is why these bourbons were able to be bottled at 107 proof. In 2009, Sazerac dropped the seven-year age statement from the bottle, leaving it as a NAS, presumably vatted from bourbons aged about six years.

Weller Antique 107 Kentucky Straight Bourbon Whiskey

FLAVOUR In the glass, Weller Antique smells of caramel, sweet cherries, toffee apple, vanilla, cinnamon and varnished wood. While the alcohol is noticeable, it isn't overpowering. The palate is rich and smooth with no heat on the tongue, but it does warm up your chest. The bourbon is sweet up front, with notes of caramel and vanilla balanced with oak. Mid-palate it is full of mixed spice and dried cherries, with a slight bitterness from the oak tannins on the back end. The finish is long. Oak tannins and dryness linger, with notes of cigar tobacco and corn. This is a very well-balanced wheated bourbon and used to be great value; allocation has made it more difficult to find, however, and retail prices have gone up. Drink it neat or on the rocks if you find the alcohol too hot, or use it to make a cocktail that needs a slightly drier bourbon.

STRENGTH
53.5% ABV (107 proof)

MASH BILL
Buffalo Trace wheated mash (16–18% wheat)

STILL TYPE
Column still

AGE STATEMENT
NAS

DISTILLERY
Buffalo Trace Distillery, Frankfort, Kentucky

BRAND OWNER
Sazerac

PRICE RANGE
$$

DRINKING RECOMMENDATION

As the popularity and hype about Pappy Van Winkle bourbon (*see* pages 147–9) have reached fever pitch, Weller 12-year-old bourbon has also become increasingly more difficult to find and more expensive. Described as the poor man's Pappy, it is made from the same wheated mash bill and aged in the same warehouses, although perhaps not on the same floors. However, due to allocation, actually finding a bottle on your local retail shelves has become near impossible so your best option for trying this bourbon is at your local bourbon bar. That being said, Buffalo Trace has invested significantly in increased production and at present has committed to not lowering the proof or dropping the age statement to increase supply. So, as supply increases, it should become easier to find in the future.

Weller Kentucky Straight Bourbon Whiskey Aged 12 Years

STRENGTH
45% ABV (90 proof)

MASH BILL
Buffalo Trace wheated mash (16–18% wheat)

STILL TYPE
Column still

AGE STATEMENT
12 years

DISTILLERY
Buffalo Trace Distillery, Frankfort, Kentucky

BRAND OWNER
Sazerac

PRICE RANGE
$$$$

FLAVOUR The bourbon has a wonderful nose of caramel, green oak and charred wood. There are also subtle aromas of vanilla and sweet cherries. The palate is smooth, semisweet and bright, with nice spice notes followed by vanilla, oak and nutmeg. The bourbon is light and approachable despite its age, and very dynamic – the whiskey goes from sweet to spice to oak in the span of three seconds. The finish has a pleasant warmth that is semisweet, with a medium body and long lingering notes of cinnamon and oak. Overall, this is a very enjoyable whiskey to drink neat.

DRINKING RECOMMENDATION

A native of San Francisco, Adam Spiegel honed his skills as a distiller at 1512 Spirit before founding Sonoma County Distilling Company in 2010. In addition to three bourbons, Spiegel produces rye and wheat whiskeys. For his West of Kentucky Bourbon No.1, he ferments a mash of yellow corn, rye and malted barley smoked with California cherry wood. The beer is double distilled in a direct-fire alembic still and matured for at least one year. While most bourbon is made on stills (pot and column) that are steam heated, Spiegel uses a direct flame. While this creates the potential for a batch to be ruined if the spirit is scorched – not unlike burning a soup or sauce on the stove – direct fire is used in Japan and Cognac for its ability to add caramelized flavour direct from distillation.

West of Kentucky Bourbon Whiskey No.1 Cherry Wood Smoked

FLAVOUR The bourbon has a lightly sweet nose with notes of wood smoke, soapstone, rye grain and oak. The palate has a very sweet and lush mouthfeel, with notes of cherry and a slightly oaky and spicey character, and a big smoke finish as you swallow. The finish is medium-long and dry, with notes of cherry, smoke and oak. This is a fascinating and unique young bourbon. It is good for those who like dry grain-forward bourbons and who also like smoke. Drink it neat or use it in a cocktail to add a great smoky character to the drink.

STRENGTH
47.8% ABV (95.6 proof)

MASH BILL
Rye mash

STILL TYPE
Pot still

AGE STATEMENT
1 year

DISTILLERY
Sonoma County Distilling Company, Rohnert Park, California

BRAND OWNER
Sonoma County Distilling Company

PRICE RANGE
$$$

DRINKING RECOMMENDATION

West of Kentucky Bourbon No.2 is made from a mash of yellow corn, wheat and malted barley. Like Bourbon No.1 (*see* page 171), it is double distilled via direct fire and matured for at least one year. Once the whiskey has reached maturity, the bourbon is vatted and bottled at 95 proof.

West of Kentucky Bourbon Whiskey No.2 Wheated

STRENGTH
47.5% ABV (95 proof)

MASH BILL
Wheated mash

STILL TYPE
Pot still

AGE STATEMENT
1 year

DISTILLERY
Sonoma County Distilling Company, Rohnert Park, California

BRAND OWNER
Sonoma County Distilling Company

PRICE RANGE
$$$

FLAVOUR This bourbon has notes of young oak and grain, followed by sweet flavours of caramel, apple and pears. The palate is very sweet and full-bodied, with notes of milk chocolate, apples, flowers and oak. The finish is long, smooth and semidry, with notes of apple skin, cocoa and oak. Although the bourbon is still young, it has nice, light fruit and floral notes balanced with oak. Drink it neat, on the rocks or in a tall cocktail for a refreshing and light summer cooler.

DRINKING RECOMMENDATION

The cask-strength expression of West of Kentucky Bourbon No.2 (*see* page 172) is made in the same way as Bourbon No.2 except no water is added to the bourbon before bottling at 110.6 proof.

West of Kentucky Bourbon Whiskey No.2 Wheated Cask Strength

FLAVOUR The nose is a little muted, but has notes of caramel followed by grain, black pepper and oak. As it breathes, light floral notes start to come out. The palate is very spicy, with notes of oak followed by light notes of vanilla and ripe pears. Despite being over 110 proof, the bourbon is very approachable. The finish is warm, dry and medium-long, with notes of spice followed by vanilla and oak. This is a big oak-forward bourbon with lots of spice and a healthy dose of alcohol to match. It is definitely a whiskey for fans of bourbons that have lots of wood character. Drink it neat, with a little water or in a high-octane cocktail.

STRENGTH
55.3% ABV (110.6 proof)

MASH BILL
Wheated mash

STILL TYPE
Pot still

AGE STATEMENT
1 year

DISTILLERY
Sonoma County Distilling Company, Rohnert Park, California

BRAND OWNER
Sonoma County Distilling Company

PRICE RANGE
$$$

DRINKING RECOMMENDATION

West of Kentucky Bourbon No.3 is made from a mash of yellow corn, malted barley and a high percentage of California rye. Like the other West Kentucky bourbons (*see* pages 171–3), it is double distilled via direct fire and matured for at least one year. Once the whiskey has reach maturity, the bourbon is vatted and bottled at 93 proof.

West of Kentucky Bourbon Whiskey No.3 High-Rye

STRENGTH
46.5% ABV (93 proof)

MASH BILL
High-rye mash

STILL TYPE
Pot still

AGE STATEMENT
1 year

DISTILLERY
Sonoma County Distilling Company, Rohnert Park, California

BRAND OWNER
Sonoma County Distilling Company

PRICE RANGE
$$$

FLAVOUR Wood and raw grain are the first things on the nose, but underlying that are notes of caramel, pear skins and a light floral character. The palate is smooth, sweet and medium-bodied, with flavours of fruit, chocolate, oak and rye spice. The finish is long, cool and dry, with the taste of ripe pear, ryebread and oak. This is a young bourbon that is very clean, has zero burn and shows lots of grain and oak character. While the whiskey lacks some complexity because of the short maturation, it is still a good bourbon for those who like more grain and oak flavours. Drink it neat or in a cocktail that needs a drier bourbon.

DRINKING RECOMMENDATION

According to legend, Thomas McCarthy, an executive at the Austin Nichols company, brought some barrel samples of bourbon with him on a wild turkey hunt. The sourced bourbon was so popular that they released it to the public in 1942 as a new brand. In 1971, Austin Nichols purchased the distillery that had been supplying bourbon for Wild Turkey, then in 1980 both companies were sold to Pernod Ricard of France. In 2009, Wild Turkey was purchased by Gruppo Campari of Italy, which invested $100 million in a new distillery, warehouses, bottling plant and visitor centre. For almost all that time, Wild Turkey 101 has been made by one man: Jimmy Russell started working at the then-called J. T. S. Brown Distillery, became the Master Distiller in the late 1960s and now works there with his son Eddie Russell.

Wild Turkey 101 Kentucky Straight Bourbon Whiskey

FLAVOUR The bourbon has an indulgent nose: creamy cherry bakewell and almond seamlessly flow into rich oak notes. There are also aromas of strawberries with sugar and cream, jammy raisin, a combination of blackberry and blackcurrant, and an underlying spiced caramel. On the palate, this starts out peppery, with notes of both baking spices and oak, before richer notes of caramel. The fruitiness from the nose also comes through, with notes of dried pineapple. The finish is full of notes of peppery rye and oak with a blackberry fruitiness on top. It is comfortingly warm, with a great note of melted butter that gradually develops into oak. Overall, this is remarkably smooth for its strength and packed full of flavour; it is fantastic served over ice, neat, straight from the freezer or in flavourful cocktails like the Mint Julep.

STRENGTH
50.5% ABV (101 proof)

MASH BILL
75% corn, 13% rye, 12% malted barley

STILL TYPE
Column still

AGE STATEMENT
NAS

DISTILLERY
Wild Turkey Distillery, Lawrenceburg, Kentucky

BRAND OWNER
Gruppo Campari

PRICE RANGE
$$

DRINKING RECOMMENDATION

First released in 2011, Wild Turkey 81 was designed by Eddie Russell to be a mixing bourbon. In general, Wild Turkey is known for doing things a little differently. For the past 60 years the Russells have maintained the same yeast strain that ferments every batch of grain. After the barrels reach maturation, which is usually about five and a half years, the barrels are vatted and bottled at either 101 proof for the flagship brand (*see* page 175) or 81 proof for this value expression.

Wild Turkey Kentucky Straight Bourbon Whiskey 81 Proof

STRENGTH
40.5% ABV (81 proof)

MASH BILL
75% corn, 13% rye, 12% malted barley

STILL TYPE
Column still

AGE STATEMENT
NAS

DISTILLERY
Wild Turkey Distillery, Lawrenceburg, Kentucky

BRAND OWNER
Gruppo Campari

PRICE RANGE
$

FLAVOUR The bourbon has a sweet nose of honey and oat cookies, with the vibrancy of lemon behind it. This develops into notes of vanilla and sweet black tea, and grows even more rich and sweet over time with notes of sweet blackberry, cherry and flaked almonds. The palate is considerably more dry and straightforward, with traditional flavours of oak and vanilla, plus a little caramelized banana that quickly fades into dry oak. The finish is relatively short, but warm at the start, with notes of creamy oak, oats and cherry. This is a smooth bourbon with a great nose but simpler, traditional palate. Enjoy it neat or with your favourite mixer.

DRINKING RECOMMENDATION

Wild Turkey Kentucky Spirit was created by Jimmy Russell as a single barrel expression of the flagship bourbon (*see* page 175). Bottled at the same 101 proof, Kentucky Spirit showcases the best barrels from the Wild Turkey warehouses that do not need to be vatted with others to find balance.

Wild Turkey Kentucky Spirit Single Barrel Kentucky Straight Bourbon Whiskey

FLAVOUR Notes of apple, vanilla and caramel are immediately noticeable on the nose, followed by very pleasant and light aromas with a hint of cinnamon, all supported by an underlying young oak. The palate is sweet with a thin body that is light and airy. Flavours of caramel and vanilla are supported by light oak tannins that give it a dry and woody character. The finish is warm, light and long-lasting. Light flavours of ripe apple and their skins give it a semidry finish with a hint of tobacco. This is a light summer bourbon to drink neat or on the rocks – despite its slightly higher proof, the light flavours might disappear in a cocktail.

STRENGTH
50.5% ABV (101 proof)

MASH BILL
75% corn, 13% rye, 12% malted barley

STILL TYPE
Column still

AGE STATEMENT
NAS

DISTILLERY
Wild Turkey Distillery, Lawrenceburg, Kentucky

BRAND OWNER
Gruppo Campari

PRICE RANGE
$$$

DRINKING RECOMMENDATION

Created by Master Distiller Jimmy Russell in 1991, Rare Breed Barrel Proof Bourbon is a snapshot of what Wild Turkey looks and tastes like straight out of the barrel. Bottled at a little over 112 proof, this is an example that illustrates Wild Turkey has consistently used a lower barrel entry proof compared to most other Kentucky bourbon distilleries who barrel their bourbon at the legal maximum of 125 proof. For the first six decades of its existence, all Wild Turkey new-make spirit went into charred new oak barrels at 107 proof. In 2004, barrel-entry proof was bumped up to 110 and then in 2006 to 115. Using a lower entry proof extracts less wood tannins and raw barrel notes, which need more time to age out.

Wild Turkey Rare Breed Barrel Proof Kentucky Straight Bourbon Whiskey

STRENGTH
56.4% ABV (112.8 proof)

MASH BILL
75% corn, 13% rye, 12% malted barley

STILL TYPE
Column still

AGE STATEMENT
NAS

DISTILLERY
Wild Turkey Distillery, Lawrenceburg, Kentucky

BRAND OWNER
Gruppo Campari

PRICE RANGE
$$

FLAVOUR The bourbon has a light nose of sweet cherries and orange zest, with a floral character resembling honeysuckle. This is followed by medium notes of vanilla and brown sugar underneath. The palate has big notes of caramel supported by deep barrel notes with a hint of fruit. The flavours are a bit nondescript due to the proof, but with a little water things open up. The finish is hot on the tongue but not harsh. While the alcohol dries out the palate, bright flavours of sweet cherries and light tobacco linger on the long finish. This is a nice high-proof bourbon with a light nose and rich caramel on the palate. If you are a fan of Wild Turkey this expression is something to look for if you want more alcohol. Drink it neat or with a little water.

DRINKING RECOMMENDATION

The Willett family have been making bourbon in Kentucky for 150 years. In 1936, after Prohibition, A. Lambert Willett and his son Thompson Willett founded the Willett Distilling Company just outside Bardstown, Kentucky. Around 1940, Willett introduced Old Bardstown Bourbon (*see* page 137) as its flagship product made from its own aged whiskey. In the early 1980s, Willett Distillery shut down its stills and re-formed as Kentucky Bourbon Distillers, working primarily as an independent bottler. In 2012 Willett installed a new 2,840 litre (750 gallon) pot still and began distilling and ageing its own whiskey once more. As Willett bourbon is just a little more than five years old, it is likely that Willett Pot Still Reserve Bourbon is made from sourced whiskey, although that might change in the future.

Willett Pot Still Reserve Kentucky Straight Bourbon Whiskey

FLAVOUR The bourbon has chocolate chip cookies with oatmeal on the nose, followed by hints of marzipan and then a green, almost vegetal oak aroma. The notes of cookies, honey and rolled oats sweeten over time, along with notes of dried apple, cinnamon, currants and a dash of fresh mint. It is rich and woody to start on the palate, then the flavour develops into richer, more buttery notes similar to those of oatmeal cookies. The finish is dry, with notes of oak, cola, spice and a light hint of mint. A flavourful, full-bodied bourbon with a pleasant sweetness, it would work well in an unsweetened Mint Julep.

STRENGTH
47% ABV (94 proof)

MASH BILL
Undisclosed

STILL TYPE
Pot still

AGE STATEMENT
NAS

DISTILLERY
Willett Distillery, Bardstown, Kentucky

BRAND OWNER
Kentucky Bourbon Distillers

PRICE RANGE
$$

DRINKING RECOMMENDATION

Founded in 2013 by Gary and Katy Hinegardner, Wood Hat Spirits is a true craft distillery making bold choices in the pursuit of flavour. Gary previously worked for a large cooperage and started the distillery while many his age are settling into their twilight years. He is a dynamo with endless creativity and determination to realise his ideas. Bourbon Rubenesque is an example of this. Not content to make a standard bourbon, Gary approaches corn like a winemaker does grapes. While all the big Kentucky distilleries use standard No. 2 yellow corn, Gary cultivates several varieties of heirloom corn grown near his distillery. Using a wheated mash with heirloom corn, Bourbon Rubenesque is matured, typically for 18 months, in 57 litre (15 gallon) barrels made from a special oak variety only used by one other distillery.

Wood Hat Bourbon Rubenesque Bourbon Whiskey

STRENGTH
50% ABV (100 proof)

MASH BILL
Wheated mash

STILL TYPE
Pot still

AGE STATEMENT
3 months

DISTILLERY
Wood Hat Spirits, New Florence, Missouri

BRAND OWNER
Wood Hat Spirits

PRICE RANGE
$$

FLAVOUR The bourbon has a bright, floral almost perfumed nose, with underlying notes of caramel and oak. The aromas are very light with a top note of green wood or grass and as it breathes a note of milk chocolate opens up. The palate is smooth and semisweet with a medium body. The bourbon is grain forward with notes of pepper spice and a light aroma of vanilla. The finish is long and has very little heat, but it is slightly sharp after swallowing. There is a pronounced dryness from the tannins, followed by lingering flavours of oak and spice. This bourbon is deceptive – the aroma is light in character, but the palate is a bit stronger and it has a big, spicy finish. But it is definitely a journey worth taking for those who like bold bourbons and a touch more alcohol. Drink it neat or use it in cocktails with vermouth.

DRINKING RECOMMENDATION

For Wood Hat's Brew Barrel Bourbon, distiller Gary Hinegardner loans used Bourbon Rubenesque barrels to a local brewery who use them to age its beer. The beer-soaked barrels are then returned and Gary finishes his Bourbon Rubenesque (*see* page 180) in the brew barrels for a short time, where it picks up additional flavour and complexity.

Wood Hat Brew Barrel Bourbon Whiskey

FLAVOUR This bourbon has nice notes of vanilla and caramel, with a hint of herbaceous aromas from the beer, followed by a pleasant backbone of oak for structure. The palate is semisweet, with a medium body and a silky texture. The flavour tastes of cooked corn, and it has a slight spicy character from the barrel. The finish has a slight warmth that is bright and lingers with a faint oily mint note, which mellows into milk chocolate and cocoa nibs. This is a really interesting non-traditional bourbon because of the small beer barrels used to finish the whiskey. Drink it neat if you like ales or more grain-forward bourbons.

STRENGTH
45% ABV (90 proof)

MASH BILL
Wheated mash

STILL TYPE
Pot still

AGE STATEMENT
3 months

DISTILLERY
Wood Hat Spirits, New Florence, Missouri

BRAND OWNER
Wood Hat Spirits

PRICE RANGE
$$$

DRINKING RECOMMENDATION

Similar to Wood Hat's Brew Barrel (*see* page 181), the Double Wood Bourbon starts its life as Bourbon Rubenesque (*see* page 180). When the whiskey has reached maturity, the bourbon is transferred from the charred new oak barrel to new small barrels made from charred pecan wood. The time the bourbon spends with the pecan wood gives it an added dimension and character not common to whiskeys only aged in oak.

Wood Hat Double Wood Bourbon Whiskey

STRENGTH
45% ABV (90 proof)

MASH BILL
Wheated mash

STILL TYPE
Pot still

AGE STATEMENT
3 months

DISTILLERY
Wood Hat Spirits, New Florence, Missouri

BRAND OWNER
Wood Hat Spirits

PRICE RANGE
$$$

FLAVOUR The nose is pleasant with notes of candied pecans and spice, followed by caramel and a faint hint of oak in the background. The palate is sweet, creamy and full-bodied, with flavours of vanilla and peaches, followed by spice and an underlying woody note. The finish is sweet and long, with notes of spice and a light nutty character followed by wood. This is a nice bourbon and, despite its youth, it is well developed. It is not over-oaked and has enjoyable complementary flavours from the pecan barrel. Try drinking it neat or in a cocktail where the pecan note can complement the drink.

DRINKING RECOMMENDATION

Montgomery County, Missouri, where Wood Hat Spirits is located, grows a variety of grains, including No. 2 yellow corn, while American white oak is milled and made into barrels just a few minutes' drive from distillery owner Gary Hinegardner's front door. To honour the work and industry of his county, Gary created Montgomery County Bourbon, which is made from a wheated mash made with yellow corn and then currently aged between 10 and 18 months (although earlier versions may have been aged to four months and the labels still reflect this), in 57 litre (15 gallon) barrels made from American white oak. After the barrels reach maturity, they are vatted and the bourbon is bottled at 100 proof.

Wood Hat Montgomery County Bourbon Whiskey

FLAVOUR The bourbon has a nice nose of vanilla and caramel and notes of oak that are spicy and vibrant. There is also a bright character almost reminiscent of Chardonnay. The palate is big, with sweet flavours of caramel and vanilla and a hint of white pepper. There is also an underlying oak character that gives the bourbon a good body and balance. The finish is warm and has lingering notes of rye spice, cocoa and oak. The finish is also dry from very subtle oak tannins. This bourbon has a more traditional profile with a bit more oak and spice due to the use of smaller barrels. At 100 proof it can be drunk neat, combined with your favourite mixer or used in a number of classic cocktails.

STRENGTH
50% ABV (100 proof)

MASH BILL
Wheated mash

STILL TYPE
Pot still

AGE STATEMENT
4 months

DISTILLERY
Wood Hat Spirits, New Florence, Missouri

BRAND OWNER
Wood Hat Spirits

PRICE RANGE
$$

DRINKING RECOMMENDATION

First introduced in 1996, Woodford Reserve Bourbon is made on the site of the 1812 Old Oscar Pepper Distillery. Brown-Forman bought the site in 1941, sold it in 1971 and repurchased it in 1993. In refurbishments Brown-Forman installed three Scottish-style pot stills as well as 100-year-old cypress wood open fermenters. Woodford Reserve Bourbon is made from vatting triple pot-distilled bourbon produced at the Woodford Reserve Distillery with column-distilled bourbon produced at the Brown-Forman Distillery. The ageing barrels are kept at Woodford Reserve between 15.5°C (60°F) and 29.4°C (85°F) year-round. When ready, they are vatted and the bourbon proofed to 90.4. In addition to the regular expression, the distillery also bottles Double Oaked Bourbon, a rye whiskey and some limited edition bourbons.

Woodford Reserve Kentucky Straight Bourbon Whiskey

STRENGTH
45.2% ABV (90.4 proof)

MASH BILL
72% corn, 18% rye, 10% malted barley

STILL TYPE
Column and pot stills

AGE STATEMENT
NAS

DISTILLERIES
Woodford Reserve Distillery, Versailles, Kentucky and Brown-Forman Distillery, Shively, Kentucky

BRAND OWNER
Brown-Forman

PRICE RANGE
$$

FLAVOUR This bourbon has aromas of vanilla, apple and caramel, with a very light, almost floral character followed by a hint of smoke and mellow oak. The palate is dry, with notes of grain and oak spice followed by some sweetness, but the alcohol is fairly aggressive on the tongue. The finish is medium-long with a sharp note of alcohol, followed by oak tannins that are dry and bright. There is also a light lingering note of apple. While the bourbon has some nice light flavours, the alcohol is fairly aggressive, but this can be mellowed with the addition of ice or when used in a cocktail.

DRINKING RECOMMENDATION

Founded in 2010 by Orlin Sorensen and Brett Carlile, Woodinville Whiskey Company has grown to be one of the most respected craft distilleries in the USA. Instead of sourcing and selling Indiana bourbon while its whiskey aged, Woodinville used a strategy of selling its whiskey in phases – initially, it offered a white whiskey, followed by a young bourbon matured in small barrels, followed by slightly older bourbon in medium-sized barrels. Today, Woodinville bourbon is pot distilled from a rye mash and aged in full-sized charred new oak barrels. The corn and rye are grown on the nearby Omlin family farm in Quincy, Washington. In 2016, Woodinville Straight Bourbon was named Best of Class Whiskey by the American Distilling Institute. In July 2017, the company was purchased by Moët Hennessy, although nothing has changed yet.

Woodinville Whiskey Company Straight Bourbon Whiskey

FLAVOUR The nose is very elegant with sweet and rich notes of vanilla, crème brûlée and rum and raisin. The palate is spicy, sweet and dry, with notes of raisin, vanilla and oak. The finish is medium-long and dry, with notes of cloves, oak and just a hint of vanilla. Woodinville Bourbon is a nice whiskey but it is also a little deceptive. While the nose is very rich and sweet, the flavour has a lot more oak and spice. That being said, it is still well balanced and would probably be enjoyed by those who like more wood-forward bourbons with touch of sweetness. Enjoy it neat, on the rocks or in your favourite bourbon cocktail.

STRENGTH
45% ABV (90 proof)

MASH BILL
Rye mash

STILL TYPE
Pot still

AGE STATEMENT
NAS

DISTILLERY
Woodinville Whiskey Company, Woodinville, Washington

BRAND OWNER
Moët Hennessy

PRICE RANGE
$$

DRINKING RECOMMENDATION

Wyoming Whiskey was founded around 2006 by Brad and Kate Mead, whose family have been in the state since 1890. The Meads decided to turn their passion for bourbon into a reality. With the help of their friend David Defazio, they commissioned retired Maker's Mark Master Distiller Steve Nally to design their distillery and develop a bourbon profile. The end result is a wheated bourbon distilled from a mash of locally grown corn, wheat and barley, aged for five plus years. Once the bourbon has reached maturity, it is bottled at 44% ABV in commemoration of the fact that Wyoming is the 44th state in the USA.

Wyoming Whiskey Small Batch Bourbon Whiskey

STRENGTH
44% ABV (88 proof)

MASH BILL
68% corn, 20% wheat, 12% malted barley

STILL TYPE
Column still

AGE STATEMENT
NAS

DISTILLERY
Wyoming Whiskey, Kirby, Wyoming

BRAND OWNER
Wyoming Whiskey

PRICE RANGE
$$

FLAVOUR Rich notes of caramel, oak and cinnamon greet you on the nose with just a touch of alcohol. The palate is semisweet, with notes of caramel and corn, followed by flavours of plums and peaches. After swallowing, the bourbon is slightly warm in the mouth with a lingering note of stone fruit and vanilla. It ends with a sweet, smooth finish and light flavours of grain and oak. This is a very fine example of a craft bourbon that is very high quality, while also working on a smaller production scale. Drink it neat or use it in your favourite cocktail for a sweeter bourbon.

DRINKING RECOMMENDATION

Yellowstone Bourbon was first introduced by Taylor & Williams as a sourced whiskey in 1872. In the 1880s, Yellowstone sourced its bourbon from Cold Springs Distillery run by J. B. Dant outside New Haven, Kentucky. After mergers with Cold Springs (in 1903), M. C. Beam (in 1910) and the repeal of Prohibition, the Dant family reopened Yellowstone Distillery at a new facility in Shively, Kentucky. Since 1944 it has been owned by Glenmore, Diageo and Luxco. In 2014, Luxco bought a 50% interest in the Limestone Branch Distillery, which presumably is distilling and ageing bourbon for the future. Located in Lebanon, Kentucky, Limestone Branch was founded in 2010 by Steve and Paul Beam, who are related to both J. B. Dant and M. C. Beam. Yellowstone Select Bourbon is currently a sourced NAS bourbon bottled at 93 proof.

Yellowstone Select Kentucky Straight Bourbon Whiskey

FLAVOUR The bourbon opens with a rich nose of vanilla and aged leather, followed by underlying notes of oak and baked apple. The palate is sweet and soft, with notes of caramel, apple and brown sugar, nicely balanced with oak. While there is some heat on the tongue, the short finish is well balanced between vanilla sweetness and oak. Yellowstone Select has pleasingly rich flavours and is not overpowering. Drink it neat, on the rocks or in most cocktails or punches.

STRENGTH
46.5% ABV (93 proof)

MASH BILL
Undisclosed

STILL TYPE
Column still

AGE STATEMENT
NAS

DISTILLERY
Undisclosed Kentucky distillery

BRAND OWNER
Luxco

PRICE RANGE
$$

DRINKING RECOMMENDATION

PART 3

THE COCKTAILS

Bourbon is a wonderful spirit that is hugely versatile – a versatility that comes from the wide range of flavours on offer, from sweet and rich to spicy and dry. While many bourbon enthusiasts love to drink their whiskey neat, on the rocks or with a few drops of water, bourbon also does a fantastic job in hundreds of classic and contemporary cocktails.

CLASSIC BOURBON COCKTAILS

Here I've pulled together 20 classic, time-honoured bourbon cocktails that offer a range of takes on the basic bourbon flavour profile, and run the gamut from tall and light to dark and complex. While almost any variety of bourbon can be used for each of these cocktails, you will find that you develop your own preferences as you drink them. For example, I like Manhattans made with a sweeter bourbon such as Evan Williams Black Label (*see* page 81), while I prefer a Highball with a drier, more grain-forward bourbon such as Larceny (*see* page 128). Your tastes may differ and you might find your favourite bourbon works better in some cocktails than others – but the experimentation is all part of the enjoyment.

A number of the recipes use a Simple Sugar Syrup. This is just one part granulated white sugar to one part water. Heat the sugar and water in a small pan and stir until the sugar is completely dissolved. Ensure that it heats to at least 60°C/140°F (a simmer). Cool and store in a sterilized bottle or jar in the refrigerator for up to 2 weeks.

In my experience, there is no correlation between the cost of a bourbon and the quality of the cocktail. However, I have found that great cocktails are always made with high-quality supporting ingredients. Good vermouth, freshly squeezed juices and fresh garnishes will pay greater dividends in your drink than splurging for a high-end bourbon and cutting corners in other places.

Short Drinks

Short drinks are cocktails served over ice in a short glass, sometimes referred to as a rocks, Old Fashioned or lowball glass. Larger versions of these glasses are called a double rocks or a double Old Fashioned.

The Boulevardier was created by Erskine Gwynne, an American writer who founded a monthly magazine of the same name in 1920s' Paris. The Boulevardier is essentially the bourbon cousin to the Negroni, though the whiskey gives the drink a different, fascinating character.

SERVES 1

Boulevardier

Add all the ingredients to a mixing glass, fill with ice and stir for about 20 seconds. Strain into a rocks glass over a large ice cube.

Twist or pinch the orange peel over the glass to express the oils, then drop the peel into the drink and serve.

VARIATIONS
Depending on your preferences and the bourbon being used, you may want to alter the balance of the drink by adding a little more whiskey: 35–45ml (1¼–1½fl oz) bourbon to 30ml (1fl oz) Campari and 30ml (1fl oz) sweet vermouth usually does the trick. You can also alter the presentation to suit – for a more elegant feel, serve the Boulevardier in a chilled coupe, or if you don't have a mixing glass, build the drink straight into a rocks glass before serving.

30ml (1fl oz) bourbon

30ml (1fl oz) Campari

30ml (1fl oz) sweet vermouth

5cm (2 inch) strip of orange peel, to garnish

The Old Fashioned Whiskey Cocktail is a version of a proto-cocktail formula first recorded in 1806 as "spirits of any kind, sugar, water, and bitters". Originally referred to as simply the Whiskey Cocktail, the term Old Fashioned first appeared in print in 1880 and was used to differentiate it from the Improved Whiskey Cocktail developed by famed barman Jerry Thomas (*see* page 194). There is much debate about whether the drink should include muddled fruit or a simple citrus peel for garnish; my suggestion is to try it with the citrus peel first before trying the muddled version.

SERVES 1

Old Fashioned

1 sugar cube

3 dashes of Angostura bitters

dash of water or soda water

60ml (2fl oz) bourbon

5cm (2 inch) of orange or lemon peel, to garnish

Put the sugar cube in the bottom of a rocks glass, add the bitters and water or soda water and muddle together. Add the bourbon and stir until the sugar is completely dissolved.

Add some ice cubes and stir again until chilled. Twist or pinch the orange or lemon peel over the glass to express the oils, then drop the peel into the drink and serve.

VARIATIONS
Variations on the Old Fashioned are endless but the primary ones are to build the drink in a mixing glass before straining it into a chilled glass over ice, substitute the sugar cube for Simple Sugar Syrup (*see* page 190) and/or use an orange wheel and maraschino cherry for garnish.

The Improved Whiskey Cocktail made its print debut in 1862, in *Jerry Thomas' Bar-Tenders Guide*, as an updated version of the Old Fashioned Whiskey Cocktail (*see* page 192). The second half of the 19th century was an inspired period in the history of the cocktail and gave birth to many of the classic drinks we enjoy today – an explosion of creative mixology that some attribute to an increased array of vermouths, fortified wines, liqueurs and bitters available in the United States at that time, allowing bartenders to blend their native bourbon with a wider range of flavours.

SERVES 1

The Improved Whiskey Cocktail

1 sugar cube

1 teaspoon maraschino liqueur

dash of Angostura bitters

dash of Peychaud's bitters

dash of absinthe

60ml (2fl oz) bourbon

5cm (2 inch) of lemon or orange peel, to garnish

Put the sugar cube in the bottom of a rocks glass, add the maraschino, bitters and absinthe and muddle together. Add the bourbon and stir until the sugar is completely dissolved.

Add some ice cubes and stir again until well chilled. Twist or pinch the orange or lemon peel over the glass to express the oils, then drop the peel into the drink and serve.

The word "toddy" is an Anglicization of a Hindi drink made from the fermented sap of palm trees. By 1786, a toddy had become commonly understood to mean a mixture of alcohol, hot water, sugar and spices. At that time, the toddy was praised as a "cure-all" and while any health claim is dubious, the mixture of warm water, honey, lemon, alcohol and spices can certainly make you feel better on a cold night or help temporarily soothe a sore throat.

SERVES 1

Bourbon Hot Toddy

Add all the ingredients to a mug, coffee cup or glass cup with a handle and stir to dissolve the honey.

Garnish with a lemon wedge. For an autumn or winter cocktail, add a cinnamon stick, if liked.

60ml (2fl oz) bourbon

15ml (½fl oz) freshly squeezed lemon juice

125ml (4fl oz) hot water

1 teaspoon honey

To garnish

lemon wedge

cinnamon stick (optional)

The Whiskey Sour dates back to at least 1870, when one of the first mentions of the drink can be found in an American newspaper. While this drink has survived for the last 150 years, its popularity has waxed and waned at various points, in part because of the widespread use of pre-made sweet-and-sour cocktail mixes. However, this easy recipe, using fresh lemon juice and sugar syrup, creates a bright, refreshing and simple cocktail that is well worth a try.

SERVES 1

Whiskey Sour

45ml (1½fl oz) bourbon

20ml (¾fl oz) freshly squeezed lemon juice

20ml (¾fl oz) Simple Sugar Syrup (*see* page 190)

To garnish

maraschino cherry

lemon or orange wedge

Combine all the ingredients in a cocktail shaker filled with ice. Shake, then strain into a rocks glass over ice.

Garnish with a maraschino cherry and lemon or orange wedge.

VARIATION
This cocktail can also be made with an egg white to give it added texture and a lovely white foam top (*see* picture opposite). If using an egg white, add all the ingredients to the shaker except for the ice and shake vigorously for 10 seconds. Open the shaker and add some ice, then shake and double-strain into a chilled cocktail glass.

The Whiskey Smash is a variation of the classic Mint Julep (*see* page 200), which can use whiskey, brandy, gin, tequila or whatever spirit you particularly fancy. We see the Smash appear in both Jerry Thomas's 1887 revised edition and *Harry Johnson's 1888 Bartender's Manual*. Over the years the specifics of how the drink is made have changed – some use crushed ice, some don't – but the basic structure of spirit, mint, sweet and sour have remained the same.

SERVES 1

Whiskey Smash

4–6 mint leaves, plus 1 mint sprig to garnish

½ lemon, cut into wedges

60ml (2fl oz) bourbon

20ml (¾fl oz) Simple Sugar Syrup (*see* page 190)

Gently muddle the mint leaves and lemon wedges in the bottom of a cocktail shaker, then fill with ice. Add the remaining ingredients, shake and double-strain into a rocks glass filled with ice.

Slap the mint sprig to release its aromatics and add to the drink to garnish.

The Mint Julep is one of the oldest American cocktails and it's still going strong. Reports from as early as 1784 show the Julep – which gets its name from the Arabic for rosewater – was used to calm upset stomachs, and Englishman John Davis noted in 1803 that Virginians liked to drink their spirits steeped with mint leaves in the morning. The Mint Julep is traditionally made with crushed ice and served in a silver cup – both of which were seen as an outward display of wealth and luxury in the 19th century.

SERVES 1

Mint Julep

2 teaspoons Simple Sugar Syrup (*see* page 190)

8–10 mint leaves, plus 1 mint sprig to garnish

60–90ml (2–3fl oz) bourbon

Add the syrup and mint leaves to the bottom of a julep cup or double rocks or Old Fashioned glass. Gently bruise the leaves with a muddler to release their oils but not so much that they break into small pieces.

Fill the cup or glass halfway with crushed ice. Add the bourbon and stir to combine the ingredients.

Top up the cup or glass with crushed ice and stir until the outside appears frosted. Add more crushed ice and garnish with the mint sprig. Serve with a short straw.

TIP
To make your own crushed ice, wrap ice cubes well in a plastic bag and a clean tea towel and crush with a rolling pin or kitchen mallet.

Drinks Served Up

Drinks "served up" are cocktails that are mixed and strained into a chilled glass with a stem, usually a Martini glass or a coupe. As a rule, cocktails of this type are never poured into the glass over ice.

The best record for the Manhattan's origin indicates that it was invented by a New York bartender named Black in the 1860s. Given the time and location of its origin, the original version probably used rye whiskey – however, bourbon Manhattans are delicious, and are my personal favourite.

SERVES 1

Manhattan

60ml (2fl oz) bourbon

30ml (1fl oz) sweet vermouth

2 dashes of Angostura bitters

maraschino cherry, to garnish

Combine all the ingredients in a mixing glass and add some ice. Stir, then strain into a chilled cocktail glass.

Garnish with a maraschino cherry.

VARIATION
For a dry Manhattan use dry vermouth instead of sweet vermouth and garnish with a lemon twist. To make a Midnight Manhattan, substitute nocino or another walnut liqueur for the sweet vermouth. The nocino adds another layer of complexity and spice that pairs particularly well with the bourbon.

This drink was created by Charles H. Baker and published in his 1939 book *The Gentleman's Companion*. The drink is named after the USS *Maine*, which sank in the harbour at Havana and was one of the sparks that started the Spanish–American War. Baker recalls creating and enjoying the drink in Havana during the 1933 Cuban Revolution. While this is traditionally made with rye whiskey, bourbon also works very well. Cherry Heering liqueur should be available from specialist drinks stores and is essential to this recipe for the additional spices that it contributes.

SERVES 1

Remember the Maine

60ml (2fl oz) bourbon

20ml (¾fl oz) sweet vermouth

2 teaspoons Cherry Heering liqueur

½ teaspoon absinthe

Combine all the ingredients in a mixing glass and add some ice. Stir for about 30 seconds, then strain into a chilled cocktail glass.

VARIATION
For a less pronounced anise flavour, try an "absinthe rinse". Pour the absinthe into a chilled cocktail glass, roll the liquid around the inside of the glass and then pour out the excess. Strain the remaining stirred ingredients into the absinthe-rinsed chilled cocktail glass and enjoy.

Created in 1924 at Harry's Bar in Paris, the drink was named for those Americans who continued to drink and flout the US Prohibition laws in place back home.

SERVES 1

Scofflaw

60ml (2fl oz) bourbon

30ml (1fl oz) dry vermouth

1½ teaspoons freshly squeezed lemon juice

15ml (½fl oz) grenadine

2 dashes of orange bitters

Combine all the ingredients in a cocktail shaker filled with ice. Shake, then strain into a chilled cocktail glass.

Flips are a class of cocktails that are frothed. Originally, pokers of red-hot iron were used to stir a mixture of beer, rum and sugar to a frothy head, although keeping a red-hot poker to hand can be problematic. By 1862 the cold flip shows up in *Jerry Thomas' Bar-Tenders Guide*, with the eggs providing a similar frothy texture.

SERVES 1

Bourbon Flip

Combine all the ingredients in a cocktail shaker with some ice. Shake thoroughly until the egg is completely combined, then strain into a coupe or other stemmed cocktail glass.

Garnish with freshly grated nutmeg.

45ml (1½fl oz) bourbon

1 egg

30ml (1fl oz) Simple Sugar Syrup (*see* page 190)

freshly grated nutmeg, to garnish

SERVES 1

Not much is known about the exact history of the Derby except that it is a very popular name for a cocktail. By 1947 there were at least three commonly accepted variations of this drink, each of which was published in the *Bartender's Guide* by Trader Vic. This recipe is known as the sour-style Derby.

Derby

30ml (1fl oz) bourbon

20ml (¾fl oz) freshly squeezed lime juice

15ml (½fl oz) sweet vermouth

15ml (½fl oz) Orange Curaçao or Grand Marnier

lime wedge, to garnish

Combine all the ingredients in a cocktail shaker filled with ice. Shake, then strain into a chilled cocktail glass.

Garnish with a lime wedge.

VARIATIONS
To make a Manhattan-style Derby, combine 60ml (2fl oz) bourbon, 1½ teaspoons Bénédictine and a dash of Angostura bitters in a mixing glass and add some ice. Stir, strain into a chilled cocktail glass and garnish with a lime wedge.

Tall Drinks

As the name implies, these cocktails are served in tall glasses over ice, with a good amount of soda, tonic or other non-alcoholic mixer, which results in a longer drink that is refreshing and less spirit-forward.

Adapted from a Scotch and Soda, the Highball became a very popular drink in the late 19th century. The name "Highball" has a much-disputed etymology, but leaving that aside, the drink itself is simple, refreshing and well worth trying.

SERVES 1

Bourbon Highball

Fill a tall glass, such as a highball or Collins glass, with ice then pour over the bourbon. Add an equal or greater part of soda water to lengthen the drink and stir. The drink should be retain the flavour of the bourbon but be lighter and refreshing.

Finish with a garnish of your choice. Try a twist of citrus peel or a maraschino cherry.

30ml (1 fl oz) bourbon

soda water, to taste

twist of citrus peel or maraschino cherry, to garnish

Sometimes referred to as a John Collins, this cocktail and the more widespread Tom Collins are essentially spirited sparkling lemonades. The John Collins first appeared in the *Steward and Barkeeper's Manual* from 1869. The original recipe called for Old Tom gin, which probably explains why the drink's name changed to the Tom Collins in *Jerry Thomas' Bar-Tenders Guide*. The Bourbon Collins is a variation on this theme.

SERVES 1

Bourbon Collins

60ml (2fl oz) bourbon

30ml (1fl oz) freshly squeezed lemon juice

20ml (¾fl oz) Simple Sugar Syrup (*see* page 190)

soda water, to top up

To garnish

orange slice

maraschino cherry

Combine all the ingredients, except the soda water, in a cocktail shaker filled with ice. Shake, then strain into a glass filled with ice.

Top up with soda water, stir and garnish with an orange slice and maraschino cherry.

A variation of the Bourbon Highball, the Bourbon Rickey was created by George A. Williamson at Shoomaker's in Washington, D.C. in 1883. The drink gets its name from Democratic lobbyist Colonel Joe Rickey, who frequented the bar and enjoyed drinking bourbon and soda on hot D.C. days.

SERVES 1

Bourbon Rickey

Fill a highball glass with ice. Squeeze over the juice from the lime half, then drop the lime into the glass and add the bourbon.

Top up with soda water and give a quick stir to mix the ingredients.

½ lime

45ml (1½fl oz) bourbon

soda water, to top up

The Daisy is a type of classic cocktail that was created in the mid-19th century. In the *Bar-Tenders Guide*, Jerry Thomas includes versions of the Daisy that can be made with brandy, gin and – as here – whiskey.

SERVES 1

Bourbon Daisy

60ml (2fl oz) bourbon

30ml (1fl oz) freshly squeezed lemon juice

1½ teaspoons grenadine

1½ teaspoons Simple Sugar Syrup (*see* page 190)

tonic water, to top up

To garnish

orange slice

maraschino cherry

Combine all the ingredients except the tonic water in a cocktail shaker filled with ice. Shake for about 20 seconds, then pour into a glass over ice.

Top up with tonic water, stir once and garnish with an orange slice and maraschino cherry.

While this is not a classic cocktail in terms of its age, its creator, Jennifer Colliau, combined two classic drinks – the Fizz and the New York Egg Cream – into something very original. Although she originally used brandy, the drink was adapted by Erik Adkins of the Slanted Door Group, and here calls for bourbon as its base spirit.

SERVES 1

Bourbon Lift

Combine all the ingredients, except the soda water, in a cocktail shaker filled with ice. Shake for about 10 seconds, then double-strain into a Fizz or Collins glass.

From about 15cm (6 inches) above the rim of the glass, pour soda water into the drink until the foam begins to bloom over the edge. Wait for a few seconds and then add a little more soda water to lift the head higher above the rim. Serve with a straw.

45ml (1½fl oz) bourbon

15ml (½fl oz) double cream (heavy cream)

15ml (½fl oz) coffee liqueur

15ml (½fl oz) almond orgeat

soda water, to top up

Punches

The word "punch" derives from the Sanskrit for the number five (pancha), since the early recipes all had five ingredients: sugar, citrus, alcohol, water and juice or tea. Punches pre-date individually prepared cocktails and are still handy for a gathering today.

While it is common to see whiskey and cola, or whiskey and ginger ale, prepared and served as an individual cocktail, the simplicity and mass appeal of a bourbon and ginger punch make it an easy crowd-pleaser to make in larger quantities.

Bourbon and Ginger Punch

SERVES HOWEVER MANY YOU WANT

1 part bourbon

2½ parts ginger ale

orange wheels, to garnish

Combine the bourbon and ginger ale in a large punch bowl, then garnish with orange wheels on the surface of the punch.

The punch can be chilled by either serving it over ice in small cups or glasses, or placing a large block of ice in the punch bowl.

While this particular recipe cannot be called a classic, the flavour that it produces certainly can, combining bourbon with apple, honey and baking spices. Freshly grated nutmeg will give a stronger flavour than ground.

SERVES 6

Bourbon Apple Punch

90ml (3fl oz) lemon juice

85g (3oz) honey

¼ teaspoon ground cinnamon

¼ teaspoon freshly grated or ground nutmeg

225ml (8fl oz) bourbon

350ml (12fl oz) unfiltered (cloudy) apple juice

8 dashes of Angostura bitters

225ml (8fl oz) soda water

To garnish

apple slices

rosemary sprig

Mix together the lemon juice, honey, cinnamon and nutmeg until well blended. Pour into a punch bowl, then stir in the bourbon, apple juice and bitters.

Top up with the soda water and garnish with apple slices and a sprig of rosemary.

Eggnog is a very popular drink with an uncertain origin and etymology. However, we do know that a drink called "eggnog" containing eggs, dairy, alcohol and sugar shows up in the American colonies around the mid-1700s. George Washington was known to serve eggnog to visitors, using a recipe that included a mix of brandy, rye whiskey, rum and sherry. Homemade eggnog can be made with any alcohol, and bourbon does a particularly nice job, especially if you use a variety that leans toward the fruity or vanilla end of the flavour spectrum.

SERVES 8

Bourbon Eggnog

6 eggs

200g (7oz) granulated sugar

½ teaspoon salt

250ml (9fl oz) bourbon

1 teaspoon vanilla extract

1 litre (2 pints) single cream (light cream)

freshly grated nutmeg, to garnish

In a large bowl, whisk the eggs until frothy. Add the sugar and salt and continue to whisk until the sugar is dissolved. Stir in the remaining ingredients.

Chill for at least 3 hours. Serve garnished with a sprinkling of nutmeg.

GLOSSARY

ABV: Alcohol by Volume

Angel's share: The portion of spirit, both alcohol and water, that evaporates from wooden barrels each year. The angel's share varies based on temperature, humidity and atmospheric pressure.

Backset: A portion of fully fermented mash held back and used to create a sour mash in a new fermentation.

Blending: When used as a legal term on a TTB-approved label in the US, this refers to the addition of neutral spirit and/or harmless blending materials, such as caramel colouring or flavouring.

Bourbon: An American whiskey made primarily from corn and aged in charred new oak barrels. The whiskey cannot be distilled above 80% ABV and must go into the barrel at less than 62.5% ABV.

Cask strength/Barrel proof: Spirit bottled without the addition of water to bring down its strength.

Column distilled: A spirit made using a column still.

Distiller's beer: Fermented mash, added to the still.

Dumped: This refers to when the contents of a barrel are emptied before further processing.

Fusel alcohols: From the German for "bad liquor", these are higher-order alcohols formed during fermentation at high temperatures, low pH or when yeast activity is limited by a lack of nitrogen. In spirits, high concentrations of fusel alcohols can produce off flavours and create a hot or harsh sensation in the mouth.

Grist: The ground-up grain solids of a mash.

Heads: The volatile and toxic compounds such as methanol and acetone that are removed from the spirit before most of the ethanol begins to volatilize.

Hearts: The centre cut of the spirit that comes off the still. This consists primarily of ethanol, water and pleasant flavour compounds.

Lincoln County Process: A required process for most Tennessee whiskey. New-make spirit is first filtered through a column of sugar maple charcoal before going into a charred new oak barrel.

Low wines: The spirit collected after the first run of a pot still. The low wines are collected and then put into the still for a second spirit run.

Mash: The mixture of grain that is cooked and fermented before being distilled.

Mash bill: The ratio of grains specific for a style of whiskey. In the case of bourbon the mash bill must consist of at least 51% corn with the other 49% from other grains.

Master Distiller: A title bestowed on a distiller who has accumulated decades of experience and knowledge producing spirits. This term is sometimes misappropriated by less experienced distillers who happen to be the more senior distiller at their company.

Neat: An unmixed spirit served without water, ice or a mixer.

New-make spirit: Newly distilled spirit that is ready to go into a barrel to mature into whiskey.

Pot distilled: A spirit produced on a pot still.

Proof: In the US proof is simply double the ABV. In the UK, 100 proof was assigned as the alcoholic strength at which gun powder, wetted with alcohol, would ignite, which is just above 57% ABV.

Proofing: The process of bringing down a spirit's alcohol concentration, usually with the addition of water or lower-strength spirit.

Pulled: When a barrel is removed from the rickhouse after reaching maturity.

Single barrel bourbon: Bourbon that has been bottled completely from one barrel.

Small batch bourbon: An unregulated term created by Kentucky distilleries. It usually refers to a whiskey that comes from the vatting of a small number of barrels (50–200 is often cited) as opposed to many hundreds or even thousands of barrels vatted for a single bottling run of one of the larger Kentucky bourbons.

Sour mash: A mash that has had its pH lowered with the addition of backset, stillage or spent beer. This makes the mash more acidic (sour) which helps the yeast to outcompete other microoganisms that might spoil the mash.

Spent beer: The remaining liquid with some residual solids after the alcohol has been stripped out.

Stillage: The leftover liquid and some solids from a distillation run.

Straight: Used to describe whiskey that has been aged for at least two years in charred new oak barrels.

Tails: The heavier fusel alcohols that come off the still after the hearts. The tails are sometimes collected and added to a striping run to extract a little extra alcohol.

TTB: US Alcohol and Tobacco Tax and Trade Bureau.

Vatting: The process of mixing (blending) spirits or barrels of spirits together.

Whiskey: An aged grain spirit. In the US there is no minimum amount of time whiskey must stay in a barrel before it can be called whiskey, however it must go into a barrel for some amount of time and in practice, the vast majority of American whiskey is at least four years old.

Whisky/whiskey: The spelling most frequently used in the US is with an "e", while the spelling without an "e" is most commonly used in the rest of the world. The TTB actually spells "whisky" without an "e", but allows the spelling with an "e" to be used as an alternate spelling on labels. Now, as to why there are two spellings for whiskey, and why the US has favoured one more than the other, this is a complicated story best described in a series of blog posts titled "Whiskey vs Whisky" on www.Ezdrinking.com.

White dog: A name given to new-make spirit, before it is aged. Sometimes white dog is also described as moonshine.

CONVERSIONS

UK	US
Autumn	Fall
Banoffee	Mixture of banana and toffee sauce
Cherry Bakewell	An open tart shell coated with a layer of preserves and filled with an almond-flavored sponge cake.
Desiccated coconut	Dry coconut
Double cream	Heavy cream
Mixed spice	Allspice
Single cream	Light cream
Soda water	Club soda
Spirit	Liquor
Sticky toffee pudding	A sponge cake with dates and covered in a toffee sauce
Top up	Top off
Treacle	Molasses
Unfiltered (cloudy) apple juice	Apple cider (sweet)

INDEX

AUTHOR ACKNOWLEDGEMENTS

I would like to thank a number of people who, without their support and inspiration, this book would not have been possible. I would like to start by thanking David T. Smith for being my friend, a source of inspiration and for pointing Octopus Publishing Group in my direction. Thank you to Sara L. Smith who supplied excellent tasting notes for 35 bourbons and Tennessee whiskeys, making the book more useful and complete. Thank you to Joe Cottington of Octopus Publishing Group for believing that I was the right author for the book and making the process so smooth.

Thanks also to the rest of the team at Octopus for collecting the bottle images, editing my prose and making this book a reality.

I would also like to thank Steve Beal, your advice and counsel at the beginning of this project made all the difference. Thank you to Bill Owens, Mike Morales and Lisa Pietsch for your encouragement. Thank you to Nancy Bramwell, Chuck Cowdrey, Eric Crizer, David Driscoll, Matthias Giezendanner, David Gouldin, Rachael Kitsch, Matthew White and Winton White, for stoking my passion for bourbon and inspiring me to be a better writer. I want to thank all of the people and companies that provided Sara and I with samples for the book. To Erik Adkins, H. Ehrmann, Nancy Fraley, Virginia Miller, Alex Pollitt,

Michael Vachon, Maverick Drinks, Master of Malt and all of the distilleries who responded to our call for help, thank you.

In particular I would like to recognize the San Francisco whiskey bars Hard Water and Elixir for allowing me to come and sample a wide range of Kentucky bourbons. Overseen by Bar Director Erik Adkins, Hard Water has an incredible wall of bourbon ranging from the everyday, craft, hard-to-find and out-of-production, as well as whiskey flights and a fantastic cocktail programme. It enabled me to track down many a bottle where I'd met dead ends elsewhere and has contributed to keeping my selection of bourbons as broad as possible. Elixir is the second oldest bar in San Francisco and is now owned by famed barman, H. Joseph Ehrmann. With more than 450 bottles of bourbon, rye, Scotch, Irish and Japanese whiskey filling its back bar and walls, it was an invaluable resource in trying and tasting my way through many a bourbon.

Lastly, I would like to thank my amazing and fantastic wife, Tia, for supporting and encouraging me while I wrote, for giving me the time to taste bourbon while we were preparing to move and for taking care of our two young boys, Giorgio and Elio. Without your help and sacrifice this could not have happened.

PUBLISHER ACKNOWLEDGEMENTS

Mitchell Beazley would like to thank all the brands and distilleries who have kindly supplied us with images to include in this book. We would also like to acknowledge and thank The Whisky Exchange, London (www. thewhiskyexchange. com) who kindly supplied the images used on pages 99, 155, 159, and 175–178.
Additional credits: 2 courtesy Angels Envy Distillery, photo Marvin Young; 7, 14 Bloomberg/Getty Images; 8ac Library of Congress, Prints and Photographs Division; 8al J Anthony Bill/Cincinnati Museum Center/Getty Images; 8ar Universal History Archive/UIG via Getty Images; 8bc Daniel Dempster Photography/Alamy Stock Photo; 8bl Photo Cuisine/Alamy Stock Photo; 8br Laurange Umbekandt/Alamy Stock Photo; 8c Bettmann/Getty Images; 8cl Jim DeLillo/Alamy Stock Photo; 8cr Emmanuel Dunand/AFP/Getty Images; 10 North Wind Archives/Alamy Stock Photo; 11, 16 Granger Historical Picture Archive/Alamy Stock Photo; 13 Library of Congress, Geography and Map Division; 17 courtesy Brown-Forman; 18, 19l Library of Congress, Prints and Photographs Division; 19r Fotosearch/Getty Images; 20 KunselmanFPG/Hulton Archive/Getty Images; 21a & b, 22a courtesy Buffalo Trace Distillery; 22b Cayce Clifford/ Bloomberg via Getty Images; 23 Gary Moseley/Alamy Stock Photo; 24 Maximilian Stock Ltd/Getty Images; 25 Laurange Unbekandt/Alamy Stock Photo; 27, 33 John Sommers II/Bloomberg via Getty Images; 28 Science History Images/Alamy Stock Photo; 29a Falkenstein/Bildagentur-online Historical Collection/Alamy Stock Photo; 29b courtesy Angels Envy Distillery; 30, 31 Karen Foley Photography/Alamy Stock Photo; 34 Daniel Dempster Photography/Alamy Stock Photo; 35 Neil Juggins/Stockimo/Alamy Stock Photo. 48, 49 Brewtography Project for Laws Whiskey House; 72, 73 Atima Bennett for Do Good Distillery; 95 Souders Studios for Golden Moon Distillery; 96, 97 Michael Wheatley for Heaven Hill Distilleries; 105 J Fix Fotoworx for Henry Farms Prairie Spirits; 162 Doyle Hudgins for Fire Oak Distillery; 165 Daric Schlesselman for Van Brunt Stillhouse; 166, 167 David Clugston for OOLA Distillery; 180–183 Garry McMichael for Wood Hat Spirits.